CW01654872

TO MAUREEN.

YOU HELPED MAKE
TODAY SO SPECIAL.
MAY GOD BLESS YOU
AS YOU READ THIS
BOOK. LET'S MARVEL
AT HIS WONDERFUL
LOVE AND GRACE.

GOD BLESS.

[signature]

Trading Punches

Fighting the Flesh, the World, and the Devil

Alistair Bates

TIMELESS
PUBLICATIONS LTD

TRADING PUNCHES

ISBN 978-0-9957886-5-7

eISBN 978-0-9957886-6-4

www.releasingcaptives.com

Published by Timeless Publications Ltd, Castlerock, Northern Ireland. www.timelesspublications.co.uk

DEDICATION

To my wife and family, who have been more loving and patient than I deserve.

CONTENTS

FORWARD

I met Alistair at my breakfast table and listened with intrigue to his journey with God. His vision excited me, so I agreed to help. Work began just a few days later with the first interview. Eventually, we recorded nearly four hours of questions and answers, which would form the basis for Alistair's publication.

As I listened, the story emerged of a man who, in common with the apostle Peter, loved God and, having let him down on a number of occasions, experienced forgiveness and restoration from the Saviour.

Alistair's memoir contains echoes of Moses's encounter with God at the burning bush (Exodus 3), where the Lord spoke directly to the Old Testament patriarch, commissioning the future Israelite leader to fulfil a task for which he felt hopelessly under-equipped. Alistair admits to feeling similarly ill prepared for the task he faced at Scrabo, until a direct meeting with God restored his passion and confidence.

In this book, we will also discover that Alistair's early days as a Christian were marked by a sense of arrogance, which was akin to that displayed by Joseph as he intimated to his eleven brothers that they would ultimately bow down before him (Genesis 37:7).

In my view, the most impressive aspect of Alistair's story is his willingness to humble himself to hear and obey God's call, even if that meant challenging previously held beliefs and being willing to change the direction of his ministry. The apostle Paul did this a number of times in response to God's prompting. (See Acts 9:3–9; 16:6.)

Trading Punches tells the story of a life saved and changed by the grace of God. It provides insight into a man who through his mistakes was humbled. Through these experiences, Alistair has emerged as a minister with a deep passion to introduce people to God. His work and witness revolutionised a declining congregation and impacted the lives of people inside and outside the church building.

For all of these reasons, I commend Alistair's book to you, fully expecting that you will be touched and inspired by his incredible journey with Christ.

Joe Boyd
Freelance Journalist

ACKNOWLEDGEMENTS

A very special thanks to Erin Brown, who has worked tirelessly as my editor and proofreader on this book. *Trading Punches* was not an easy book to write, as I tried to balance personal narrative with biblical truth. Erin provided insight, spiritual awareness, and motivation, without which, this book may not have been published. I look forward to many more projects together. *Trading Punches,* was birthed from a series of interviews with Joe Boyd, a freelance journalist. Joe was convinced there was a story to tell, and I thank him for the motivation he provided for me.

INTRODUCTION

A champion is someone who gets up—when they can't.
Jack Dempsey

As I sat in the minister's study at Scrabo Presbyterian Church putting on my hand wraps, I wondered whether the office had ever been used as a preparation area for a charity exhibition boxing match. Probably not.

The opening notes of "The Mighty Quinn" announced my opponent, professional boxer Stevie Quinn, as he entered the ring. A short time later I emerged to strains of "Tubthumping" by Chumbawamba. I hoped its chorus, "I get knocked down, but I get up again," would not be prophetic.

Packed into the church car park, a rambunctious crowd of about 400 or 500 people cheered. It was the finale to a Community Celebration Day organised in partnership with the Westwinds Development Association, known to be a tough housing area. The bright blue canvas beneath my feet mirrored the cloudless sky. The faint ripple of air that caressed my skin would not be enough to fill my lungs in the heat of battle. I tried not to be distracted by some of the elderly who filled the VIP seats at ringside—members of my congregation. Whether they were chanting "Quinn" or "Bates" I was not sure!

My heart thudded against my rib cage, and in my head its noise echoed above the din of the crowd. Exhibition or not, punches hurt and I wanted to avoid embarrassment.

It seemed like an eternity before the bell sounded for the first round. I gripped my gum shield tight as if to weld it into place. Quinn and I moved to the centre of the ring and exchanged opening blows. He was toying with me, yet we both succeeded at landing some punches. I was conscious that male pride could take us to places I didn't want to go. One punch delivered with enough force could end up with our trading damaging punches. And the only health in danger would be mine!

The second round seemed to last forever, as it had not been timed accurately. The long walk back to my stool felt like a marathon rather than just a few steps.

We emerged for the final round, touched gloves, and exchanged our final few punches. Mercifully, the ending bell sounded and the action stopped with me against the ropes. My arms and legs felt like jelly. I could hardly breathe. But I was still standing! Whilst I boxed in only an exhibition bout against a superior opponent, I had managed to stay on my feet —certainly proof of my hidden talent.

Yet every day an intense and brutal battle rages. A must-win battle, with everything at stake! That battle ends with just one winner, and the victor will be declared as the one still standing.

Daily each one of us is involved in a contest against our flesh, the world, and our greatest Enemy—the devil. Though we will cover these more thoroughly throughout the book, for now let's briefly look at these three opponents to our Christian walk.

Simply put, our flesh is our rebellion against God. The apostle Paul suggests that the flesh remains weak even after putting our trust in God. We still have our vulnerabilities and flaws we must work through. Often as Christians our struggles are no longer against the obvious sins (lying, cheating, drunkenness, and the like) but against the hidden desires of our hearts: The craving to have others consider us successful may compound our sense of personal failure. The desire to be loved intensifies our experience and fear of rejection. The need for human relationship, a God-given characteristic, when distorted by our weaknesses leaves us struggling to manage loneliness. The book you're holding will not ask you to deny, or even lament, your weaknesses but to use them as an opportunity to depend more on God, to lean heavily on him when you feel like your weaknesses are taking over your life.

When we overcome the flesh, when we trust God, our weaknesses are turned on their heads. The fear of failure no longer drives us to be successful, but success enables us to help others, which becomes our strongest motivation. When ripped apart by our brokenness, love fuels self-indulgence and desperation. Not so when liberated by the Spirit. Sanctified love enables us to love when there is not much in the way of return. The craving for human relationship is less about having a friend and more about becoming a friend.

When human needs are governed by "the flesh", we often become high maintenance. We spend most of our day wanting other people to attend to us, when, in fact, the Bible requires us to provide for the needs of others. It's about using those broken moments in our lives as stepping-stones to recovery; however, this happens only when they can be used in the process of helping others to heal. If we cannot overcome the weakness of human flesh, then we cannot inspire or offer hope to others. We boast in our weaknesses only to the extent that God was our strength during such times, and that God will be their strength too.

The world we live in is not our home. Its corrupted and broken structures should cause us not only to lament its condition but also to compel us to engage those who live in it —to love others in the way that Christ did. Yet the manifestation of such love and concern is difficult to find. Many hearts are baked hard in the heat of daily existence. Living on this broken planet is like a perpetual drought without the summer rains. Life is hard. Communities are torn apart by war and strife. Refugees flee the bloodshed, and children are sold for pennies. Spouses who once walked the isle to say "I do" now stand in law courts saying "Never again." Besieged by debt, crippled by self-doubt, and lost in loneliness, we find this world to be a tough place to live in.

But our battle is not against those who live in it; rather, we must focus on what breaks the world. To wage war against the world's corrupted systems is a battle worth fighting and a war worth winning. God extends his day of grace for that very reason. He tolerates its brokenness because he overwhelming loves the broken people living within it. We must pour ourselves into this world with an aspiration to win it to Christ.

Our greatest Enemy, therefore, is not human weakness or even the broken structures of a planet in decay; rather, our Enemy is the one who seeks to destroy our world and everybody in it. The devil is intent on eliminating our effectiveness as individual Christians as well as the collective entity of Christ's church. He wants the church to be distracted and divided so that we see one another as opponents rather than him as our genuine opposition.

He wants to undermine and disable our confidence and trust in God, so he reminds (accuses) us of our failures. He whispers, "God can't use failures; therefore, he won't use you." Satan cannot accept his own rejection, so he will exploit ours, trying to get us to avoid God. He perpetuates the lie, "If others cannot accept you, why do we believe God could?" The beauty of relationships eludes the devil, who will suffer eternal loneliness, so he wants others to feel that they have been abandoned too. This thief of all that is holy has only one intent for all of humanity made in the image of God: to steal, kill, and destroy.

Why do we need to trade punches with the flesh, the world, and the devil? Simple. The devil is the inspiration behind the exploitation of our weaknesses and the broken structures of this world. If we stay vulnerable, we never find our strength in God. If we always want out of this world, we lose sight of those spiritually dying in it. If we make our enemies others, we will never see the real Enemy, who was thrown out of heaven because of his arrogance and desire to be God rather than to serve him. If we do not train to fight this great opponent, we will only ever be fighting ourselves and one another. It is necessary then that we confront our own shadows and the brokenness of this world so that we are better equipped to fight our real Enemy. Remembering that we fight not against flesh and blood will take us all into the arena of the last and most important battle: the destruction of the Evil One.

Will our Christian lives and ministries be standing at life's final bell? By God's grace we can shout a firm yes! God has not left us alone in the ring of life to spar with our opponent. Not only must we learn from our mistakes, but also we must strategically build a defence against the Enemy. And God has provided us with the means of victory:

> What causes fights and quarrels among you? Don't they come from your desires that battle within you? You desire but do not have, so you kill. You covet but you cannot get what you want, so you quarrel and

> fight. You do not have because you do not ask God. When you ask, you do not receive, because you ask with wrong motives, that you may spend what you get on your pleasures.
>
> You adulterous people, don't you know that friendship with the world means enmity against God? Therefore, anyone who chooses to be a friend of the world becomes an enemy of God. Or do you think Scripture says without reason that he jealously longs for the spirit he has caused to dwell in us? But he gives us more grace. That is why Scripture says:
>
> "God opposes the proud
>   but shows favor to the humble."
>
> Submit yourselves, then, to God. Resist the devil, and he will flee from you. Come near to God and he will come near to you. Wash your hands, you sinners, and purify your hearts, you double-minded. Grieve, mourn and wail. Change your laughter to mourning and your joy to gloom. Humble yourselves before the Lord, and he will lift you up.
>
> James 4:1–10

Our Enemy is relentless and brutal in his attacks. We must move forward in attack if we hope to win, for retreat is certain defeat. If we learn to stand firm fully submitted to God, then we will have the reward of hearing the final bell. If we deploy well, victory will be secured.

As you read *Trading Punches*, you'll see through my mistakes, doubts, fears, and failings how faithful God was to his calling to me—just as he is faithful to his calling for you. We are all on a journey to a deeper walk, a richer faith in God. I hope your fears will give way to confidence as you realise that the Coach in your corner is the greatest of all time, Jesus Christ.

PART ONE: THE FLESH

What causes fights and quarrels among you? Don't they come from your desires that battle within you?

James 4:1

Wars rage on mountainsides, in valleys, and on desert plains. The noise of conflict is never distant, and the tragedy of war fills blogs, articles, and newsreels. The ethics of war are debated in classrooms, the tactics of war scrutinised by politicians. The reality of human conflict is the subject of poets and novelists.

However, not every battleground is discernible to the naked eye. Some conflicts lie deep beneath the surface, within our hearts and minds. Some days we feel our inner conflicts raging out of control. At other times we smile, as if we have triumphed. James reminds us that the flesh is a very real enemy. Living in the flesh is not just about possessing skin and bones; rather, it's about our desires, impulses, and motivations, which without God are a destructive enemy.

My journey may be different from yours. However, as you travel with me, you will be surprised by our similarities. Separated by land and sea, we are joined together with the bonds of common humanity. Our terrain might be different, but we are fighting the same battle. What matters is not where the war is fought but how we fight it. Together we can subdue the flesh and bring our desires, impulses, and motivations under the controlling power of God's Holy Spirit.

> Therefore I do not run like someone running aimlessly; I do not fight like a boxer beating the air. No, I strike a blow to my body and make it my slave so that after I have preached to others, I myself will not be disqualified for the prize."
>
> 1 Corinthians 9:26–27

CHAPTER ONE

First Steps

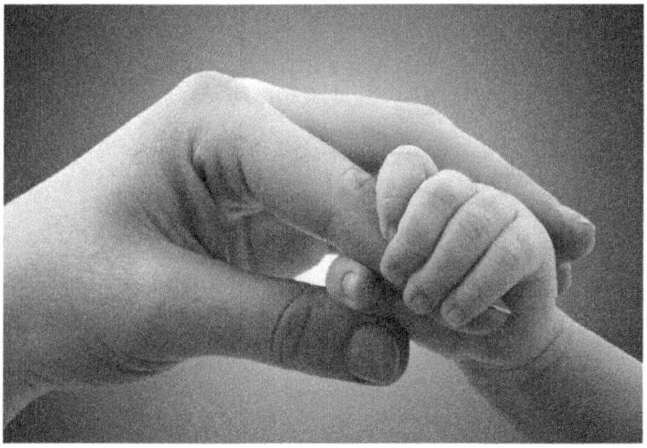

Beatlemania came to the townland of Finaghy, Belfast, in November 1964 when John Lennon, Paul McCartney, George Harrison, and Ringo Starr took to the stage at the King's Hall as thousands of teenagers screamed with excitement.

Earlier that year, I was born in the same district but with much less fanfare. My father, Meredith Bates, was a former RAF serviceman who hailed originally from Groggan, near Randalstown. My mother, May, was a native of the

Donegal Pass area, Belfast.

After his military service ended, we moved back to Randalstown, while I was still in primary school.

My first memories centre on the death of my grandmother. She lived upstairs in the back bedroom. I was only three when she died. I recall my mother in floods of tears and obviously distressed at her passing. Now all these years later I realise why. The day my parents buried my grandmother they got news that my grandfather had suddenly passed away too. At three years of age I sensed vulnerability even if I could not articulate it. Watching the distress of my parents etched within me a chilling memory.

Tears and anxiety broke into my life as the unwelcome visitor rather than the invited guest. As a child I was never strong enough to resist their bully advances. My first day at primary school began with me in tears because I didn't want to go. My state must have distressed my brother, for he stood on the stairs, pleading with my mum not to send me. But my tears and his pleading fell on deaf ears.

I don't think I ever wanted to be at Finaghy Primary School. In fact, I would rather have been stranded on the moon than walk up the school path. My painful memories were fuelled by one particular incident. I was eight at the time and sat beside the class clown. The days he made me laugh were the days worth going to school. On this particular day, the teacher had slipped out for a moment. Though this young, tall, athletic teacher was inexperienced in the classroom, he certainly was an imposing character. He returned just as I chuckled at my classmate's antic. He called me up to the front of the class and motioned me towards his desk. Without a word, our tutor lifted me by the scruff of the neck to his full height and then dropped me onto his chair. Unknown to me, someone had positioned seven or eight drawing pins pointing upward on the chair. As I landed on these small weapons, they stuck in my leg. I shot up from the chair and frantically tried to remove them. Eventually, speckles of blood stained my fingertips. The teacher then banged my head off the Portakabin wall. He thought I was responsible for placing the drawing pins on his chair, intending for him to feel the pricks of pain. The head banging was his way of dealing with the situation.

The negative impact from this experience was both immediate and long lasting. He spent the rest of the year finding ways to humiliate me in front of the class. At least in my newfound sensitivities that is how I interpreted each event.

On one occasion, he asked a girl to read out a poem she had written. In one verse, she talked about pylons walking across the fields. He looked at me and asked, "Do they walk?"

I didn't know what pylons were, so I said, "Yes, they do."

He laughed at me and the whole class joined in. What likely appeared innocent to them was slowly but surely crushing my confidence.

Later that year we held a Mastermind quiz. My subject was astronomy because I had always liked to read about our solar system. I was very young when Neil Armstrong walked on the moon, and it had fascinated me. While taking the quiz I froze at some of the questions. At this, my teacher subsequently said to the class, "Well, Alistair obviously doesn't know as much as he thinks he does."

As the humiliation continued, I effectively shut down, unable to apply myself to my studies. That year, and for many years to come, I would open my school books and stare at the page. When it was time to sit the eleven-plus, the principal advised my parents to withdraw me from the exam, believing I would not succeed. But they made me do it anyway. The headmaster's plea was indeed prophetic, for I failed the exam.

My parents died before I had the opportunity to talk to them about this incident, as I had hidden the hurt in my heart. But it is only now as a parent that I realise that they were never disappointed in me but only what was happening to me. At the time, I felt hurt that they had not protected me from further humiliation. Yet, how were they to know of my pain and mortification? I had never articulated such feelings and they had never asked. Back then children were to be seen and, unfortunately, not heard.

Today the Internet has opened up a door that is difficult to close. As the relentless tide of comments, likes, dislikes, images, and suggestions mould the minds of our children, it is critical that we listen to their perceptions and opinions, and not shut the door on their emotions. Pull back from the noise and mayhem and ask them how they feel. Be a listening presence in their lives. Take a step into their world now so that one day they can take a step into the safety of yours.

Yet every cloud has a silver lining, and failing the exam did have its benefits. It meant that I would attend Randalstown High School. The teachers and students there were fantastic. My cousins attended the school. Even though I wasn't progressing academically, I enjoyed the interaction with some of the teachers. One in particular, Thomas Allen or "Cammie" Allen, as we called him, sought to encourage me. When necessary he would chastise us students; however, he was fair in its administration. But, more important, he always encouraged each pupil when he found something commendable. Mr. Allen never humiliated me. In fact, he had a sarcastic wit that I enjoyed.

The school was at the centre of a village, where everybody knew one another. Residents shared a real feeling of togetherness in what were still very difficult times for the province. The Troubles were at their height, yet our village shared solidarity and a strong sense of community. I enjoyed those days until I turned fourteen and left to attend Antrim Technical College.

My childhood was a mix of pleasant summer days and dark, troubled emotions. As an escape from the city of Belfast during the Troubles, or what would be known elsewhere as a civil war, my family spent time at a caravan park. There it felt like we were a million miles away from the bombs and bullets. Children, both Protestant and Catholic, played together in a way they would not do at home. Football in the park, table tennis, and midnight swims made summer seem to stretch into forever. Each of my aunts and uncles had a caravan close by, so we shared a distinct togetherness. The Troubles had done much to alienate two warring communities, but, ironically, those two very separate communities each had found greater cohesiveness and solidarity within itself. Protestants forged strong bonds with one another, as did their Catholic counterpart. Perhaps that's why Irish Catholics throughout the world have a strong sense of community.

I never wanted the summers to end, but, sadly, they always did. I was always subdued on the journey home from the caravan park.

As a child it seemed easier to adjust to bombs, bullets, and hatred than it did to personal fear, anxiety, and worthlessness. I had an evolving hatred of the "other side" and found reasons to justify my anger. In looking back, my increasing sectarianism probably gave me something worth living for, a dangerous distraction from my own emptiness. I had left primary school, but primary school had not left me. My experiences there affected all of my compulsory education years. I left every educational institution with a blank sheet of paper rather than a certificate of qualifications. I was sixteen years old and had nothing to show for all the time spent in classrooms. The crowds that I laughed with in the day were not the same troublesome thoughts that visited me at night. Their unwelcomed conversations were difficult to ignore. They reminded me of my loneliness and took great delight in highlighting my failures. They spoke of my past and mocked my future. Those unkind voices travelled with me during the night and stalked me in the shadows during the day. Some nights would have been easier not to wake up from, and yet I learned to cope. I forged the capacity to adjust to each and every set of changing circumstances.

As we age, we are tempted to lose the resilience developed in childhood. For all the criticism of young people, we understate their adaptability. They learn to cope with life and change in a way that adults refuse to. As a pastor I am confronted with adults who get buried in their circumstances.

Overwhelmed and seemingly overpowered, they are tempted to give up. If this is where you are, let me remind you not to give up hope. God has plans to prosper you and not harm you. His plans include not only your survival but also your revival and personal renewal. His infusion of grace and strength will compensate for what you lack.

The truth is, without God, no matter how adaptable we were as children and young adults, we will one day dissolve. The relentless punishment of the Enemy traps us against the ropes and eventually nails us to the canvas, unable to beat the count. In the words of Isaiah 40:30, "Even youths grow tired and weary, and young men stumble and fall." Yet, the canvas forces us to look in a different direction: upward. In spiritual terms, the view from the canvas should enable us to see God. The next verse continues, "But those who hope in the Lord will renew their strength" (v. 31) and, "He gives strength to the weary and increases the power of the weak" (v. 29). If you are looking in the right direction, you will receive what the self-sufficient miss: an infusion of God's grace, strength, and power. To beat the count requires a certain type of disposition, an attitude and perspective that you alone bear responsibility for. And it is this: the canvas is not your final resting place. To rise to your feet, you will have to trust, regardless of what you feel and see, that God has not abandoned you.

Of course, I had still a few miles to travel before my own personal deliverance, and with ever decreasing options I went to the government training centre in Ballymena to "serve my time" as an apprentice engineer.

Fighting continued on the streets of Belfast but now

the enemies were even closer. I left a Protestant school because our education system was segregated. We often lived in a predominately Protestant housing area where some had the luxury of working in Protestant or Catholic businesses. The government training centre in Ballymena had a mix of Protestants and Catholics, and some days standing beside one another forced many of us out of our comfort zones. We may have looked the same, but we were still defined by colour—the Protestant flag was red, white, and blue; and the Catholic flag, green, white, and gold. We painted our tribal colours on walls and sidewalks and conducted territorial parades. The apostle James was right. We had "fights and quarrels among [us]" (James 4:1). A conflict bereft of a political solution.

Yet hidden away from view another war was raging, one that never made the headlines. It was so epidemic, so contagious that it had the power to cross every national boundary. A silent war, a subversive campaign. Its victims suffered hidden wounds untreatable by conventional medicine. It was the relentless war erupting deep in the heart of every human being. Its daily onslaught was rendering me defenceless. My visible collapse was the result of what James describes as "the desires that battle within you." But I was not the only one engaged in this battle, for we all have desires within that battle against us.

Before I could deal with a broken world, I had to deal with a broken me. That's the problem with human brokenness, the enemy is often staring back at us in the mirror. And without God, we cannot win the battle. God has created us for recognition, acceptance, and approval. However, the Enemy takes us to the wrong people and places to find them. Our flesh is high maintenance. It is addicted to the only life it knows: self—self-indulgence, self-satisfaction, selfish longings and desires. But the more it feeds on its desires, the less it is satisfied. Flesh's power needs to broken.

I was pushing the limits of the plastic ruler of my life, and it was about to break. I was soon to learn how fragile I actually was without God.

CHAPTER TWO

Trying to Stand Alone

Church was central to our family life. After all, we are Irish . . . well, British, or maybe Anglo-Irish—it's great to be able to change identity when it suits. My father was an elder in the Presbyterian church in Finaghy and then in Second Randalstown Presbyterian. He served as a lay preacher as well, and always thought through every theological issue. Mum was a devout Christian and a great prayer warrior.

Though brought up in the church, by the time I reached my teens, my older siblings were no longer attending, and I wasn't long behind them. At fourteen I stepped away from church, not wishing to look back. However, the church's teaching wasn't so quick to release me and had a way of robbing me of the enjoyment I sought.

When I left school without qualifications and attended the government training centre, it quickly became apparent that I wasn't succeeding there either. I couldn't fit in as an apprentice engineer, and I had no intention of pursuing engineering as a career.

I spent many nights in Antrim at the Rollerdrome. In those days roller discos were the big thing. I went there mainly to meet girls and listen to music. An occasional fight livened up the night as well.

Life at home was becoming strained with my parents. I had left the church, I was staying out at night, and they didn't like the company I was keeping. They worried about me intensely, demonstrated by my mum's attempt to curtail what I was doing. But I only added to their anxiety when I showed signs of being influenced by the Troubles. Hate toward what was called the "other side" grew within me. I erected sectarian images and emblems in my bedroom and listened to political songs. I needed a cause, a reason for living. I sought it anywhere other than where my parents had found it—in lives dedicated to serving the Lord.

A confrontation with my parents one evening was so bitter and emotionally charged that I prepared to walk out the door, cutting them out of my life and never seeing them again.

In their wisdom, seeing the bigger picture of our relationship, they stepped down, and in doing so kept their son. Looking back, I can't help but wonder if they saw through my pretence of being stable, perceived that I was fragmenting on the inside, and in faith released me into the Lord's care.

How the flesh builds its defences against godly correction! I was reacting against the truth because I was blinded by ingrained perceptions about myself and the world around me. As I reflect upon that period in my life, I find Steven Porter's analysis of *sarx* (flesh) helpful;

> The relational resistance view maintains that σάϱξ is not simply ingrained inclinations to behaviourally sin, but more fundamentally ingrained inclinations to resist the Spirit of God and to live autonomously from his life-giving presence. . . . To put the point another way, what stands in the way of progress in holiness is not merely σάϱξ understood as the Christian's habituated desire to sin, but σάϱξ understood as the Christian's habituated desire to be one's own god.

Porter writes this passage with reference to the Christian's struggle with sanctification. Yet it perfectly describes the war that was raging in my heart. My will and desire to change was fundamentally disabled, and it was based on a deeply ingrained conflict with God. My interpersonal issues needed to be resolved. Resisting the advances of the Holy Spirit, I kept anyone representing God at arm's length. Fighting my parents as well as attempting to find a life apart from God was, in one sense, killing me.

I was chasing dreams that life without God was much more preferable. It is what Gregory Boyd describes as "the grand illusion of the flesh." In his book *Present Perfect,* he writes:

> It's the main obstacle that keeps us from finding true life. Our minds are blinded by "the god of this age" (2 Corinthians 4:4) so that we keep living as though what is true is false and what is false is true. When we live as though we were lords of our own life, capable of meeting our own needs, we are living in the flesh. When we treat people, possessions, or achievements as though they were the source of our worth and significance rather than God, we are living in the flesh. In fact, insofar as we live as though God were not present, moment-by-moment, and as though this wasn't the most important aspect of any present moment, we are living in the flesh.

I ran after everything but God while my parents watched helplessly. It is difficult for godly parents to let go of their children and let God pursue them. I cannot help but think of the Father waiting for the prodigal son to return. Had I been that father, I would have been tempted to chase after my son, rewrite the script, and hasten the happy ending. Yet the Father stood waiting. Jesus used the parable because in popular Jewish theology borders defined the presence of God. This son was not fit to worship because he tended unclean animals, worked in Gentile territory, and lived outside the influence and reach of God. Yet that is the very place where the son came to his senses and God brought him home. Maybe you are a parent reading this today and God is asking you to trust him in the same way. I thank God my parents did.

The battle with my parents and the mundane familiarity numbed my soul. The group of teenagers I hung out with often assembled at the Protestant summer seat that divided our town. One evening I stood among my friends who were talking and joking with one another. But I felt overwhelmed by emptiness, disconnected from everything. I sensed that nothing mattered anymore. Something within me was broken and I couldn't fix it—I couldn't even identify it. This awareness of powerlessness filled me with fear. I had nothing to aspire to. My life was empty, void of anything meaningful or worthy of pursuit.

I had friends who accepted me as one of their own, but not even that made me happy. I was lonely and isolated. I just felt that I didn't belong to this world. When I considered what the future might hold for me, questions swirled in my head: Why bother? Why be here when I don't have anything to live for? I have no qualifications, no trade, in fact, no anything.

I contemplated answers to my questions, trying to determine what I should do. Then, without telling any of my companions, I left. I set off walking through the village. Where I would end up, I wasn't sure.

CHAPTER THREE

Searching for Happiness

It's ironic how loneliness intensifies when daylight fades. My footsteps echoed against the still summer's night. I set off with no particular destination in mind. I just knew I couldn't stay where I was. In the distance was the stone graveyard attached to the church that my parents attended. I felt that those encased in the soil beneath the foreboding gravestones had more life than I currently possessed.

As I trudged up the Portglenone Road, I recalled that Tony and Valerie McGall had rented a house close to the church. They, along with Campbell and Clare McMaster, had been my youth leaders in Second Randalstown, where I had attended as a young teenager. I hadn't seen them for a few years.

Without consciously planning my route, I ended up at their front door. Questions raced through my mind. What would Tony and Valerie say when they opened the door and saw me standing there? What if they felt obliged to invite me in without really wanting me there? Could I face another rejection? Did they still host a Bible study for young people on Friday nights? What if everyone I had known had moved on? Would I be sitting in a roomful of strangers?

I summoned every ounce of courage and lifted the door knocker. As it left my grasp, the loud bang shattered the silence. I lingered, unsure of what to expect. As the door slowly opened, Tony's eyes caught mine, and as recognition flashed across his face, he smiled. "It's great to see you, Alistair. Why don't you come in?"

I went in and discovered they, indeed, still held Friday night Bible study. I found a seat in the living room. I watched and listened as the group of young people talked about God as if he were their friend, a God whom I didn't possess, a God whom I had no experience with. To this day I can't recall their words or remember a single detail of their conversations. The Bible passage we studied is a mystery, as is Tony's kindness to me at the door that night. But upon reflection, I think the Spirit of God made me sensitive to their sense of peace, love, and spiritual certainty, for that is what I remember with crystal clarity. They appeared to have everything I lacked. And rather than helping ease my pain, their expressions of what I lacked made it even worse.

After saying good-bye to Tony and Valerie that evening, I returned home. All alone in my bedroom I sat. Even though the bedroom light was on, darkness shrouded me. A palpable sense of futility descended on me. Every negative thought pierced my heart with machine-gun repetition. I felt my heart would cease retaining anything of value. That night the pain was almost insufferable. My despair was unbearable.

As the war raged in my heart, my flesh refused to give up without a fight. That night the Holy Spirit allowed my pain, loneliness, despair, and futility to draw me to submission. When you fall on your back, there is only one place to look. And that is up!

I had known from childhood that Jesus declared he was the way, the truth, and the life, but I had convinced myself that I could find all of those things without him. The real truth was, I couldn't. I was at a crossroads: continue in my present misery, or submit to God.

I was still attending the government training centre (GTC), and I thought, "Lord, you have got to change me because if you don't, I have no future. I am broken and I cannot fix myself. I have fouled up. Not only have I sinned against you, I have sinned against myself and my own family, for they are despondent about my future." I paused before adding, "Lord, I am really reluctant to do this because I have friends in the training centre, including one particular friend, and he's a punk."

I couldn't remember the last time I prayed, but that night I couldn't seem to stop. "Lord, my becoming a Christian means I must say good-bye to some of these friendships, but some of them are what have kept me alive. Those friends stopped me from ending it. They gave me some reason for getting up in the morning. If I follow you, they will no longer want to be part of my life. Monday morning I'll walk into GTC and be alone again, just as I was so many years ago. I can't really sacrifice that, even though I know it is what I need to do."

I painfully reflected on this, knowing that regardless of the battle within my heart, to live life without God was no longer an option. "Lord, I have got to become a Christian. I know this and I haven't the strength to fight it any longer. You have got to become my future for me." I swallowed hard. Accept me now. I need Your forgiveness. I need you to take hold of my life and forge a pathway for my future."

After I prayed that prayer, I wasn't sure how I would tell everyone that I had become a Christian. I was seventeen and insecure, afraid of what others would say about my "conversion" I decided, "I am not going to tell anyone I am a Christian. I am going to let them see that I am not swearing or doing the things that I once did."

The next morning I woke up sick. In fact, I felt ill for a week and couldn't attend my classes at GTC. It seemed ironic that the previous night I had given my life to Jesus and now I couldn't get out of bed because I was ill. Looking back, I believe God permitted that period of sickness. It gave me time to talk to God without human interruption. Perhaps if I had not been forced to languish in bed, the voice of others would simply have drowned out his.

Even at that, upon my return to work I didn't tell my punk friend for a couple of weeks. I thought that if he knew I'd become a Christian, he would tell everybody else, mock me, and try to humiliate me, even though I was his friend. When I eventually told him, he looked at me and said, "That's okay. That's fine if it is what you want to do, as long as you don't expect me to do the same. You choose what you want to choose."

I didn't lose his friendship. In fact, our relationship deepened. We enjoyed a growing respect for each other, and whilst he didn't believe in my newfound faith, he agreed that I should at least follow it. He accepted our differences.

His favourable reception bolstered my confidence to tell other people that I had become a Christian. My zeal blossomed to the degree that I graffitied the toilets at GTC with Scripture verses! Alongside the profanities and swearwords, I scribbled Bible verses. I was so passionate about my decision to follow Christ that my work colleagues dubbed me Batesie the Bible Thumper.

For years I had sought the approval of others. And each time I didn't receive it, a little piece of me died. I wanted everyone to love me. That is, everyone except God. The day that the drawing pins on my teacher's chair pierced my skin, humiliation pierced my heart. Every perceived negative comment, even mild criticism, hung over me like a dark cloud. A young child's life is rich and tender soil, and whatever is planted in it, good or bad, takes root. And on that day in particular I became conscious of my inner brokenness.

Born broken and spiritually disorientated, we have

little resistance to the hurts caused by others. The problem is, without God we attempt to repair what is broken within us. Such efforts are marked by exhaustion, disappointment, and, often, a silent resignation of failure. Or, perhaps worse, we create a delusion that we have succeeded, producing pride that even our families find difficult to tolerate. Yet I was under no such illusion. Failure had marked my life both privately and publicly. I have been floored in the boxing ring, but even that was less painful than dealing with my day-to-day brokenness. However, I have never been very good at saving myself—actually, no one has been able to save themselves. I thought that my deliverance to deserved happiness would come through every friend I made, every girlfriend I loved, every person I hated. I had nailed myself to the cross, but my wounds just left me bleeding and never redeemed.

And this is the flesh's lie: it leads us to believe we are the master of our own destiny. Its power of deception is that life can be lived in God's absence. That night alone in my bedroom, I finally discovered that it could not. For years I had been running away from the One who could save me. But at seventeen, I ran directly into his arms.

At Calvary, Jesus's flesh was torn so that ours could be disarmed. On that memorable night 2,000 years ago, Jesus broke the stranglehold of sin and set us free from the power and penalty of sin.

Once I believed God and accepted his redemption, no longer did I have to make something of my life. For the first time God was in charge. I had spent the first seventeen years pursuing happiness, only to feel bitterly disappointed with my efforts. Now that God was gaining control of my life, he became responsible for its shape and direction.

We are often told you can't choose your family but you can choose your friends. When God is in charge he chooses your friends too!

CHAPTER FOUR

Friends Who Stood with Me

In my late teens, Tony and Valerie McGall, as well as Clare and Campbell McMaster, had an amazing influence on me. They helped lay the building blocks of spiritual development, affording me a deep and lasting passion for the Bible.

The McGall's and McMaster's homes and lives were always open to young people. In addition to their Friday evening youth Bible studies, Tony and Valerie ran the Youth

Fellowship on Sunday evenings. The discussions, often intense and inspiring, gravitated to the Bible and our experiences of God. Oftentimes, Tony played devil's advocate. He would make a controversial statement, and we would have to search the Bible and browse commentaries either to challenge or validate his claims. Many of those Friday Bible studies lasted for hours, sometimes until after midnight. The quest to study Scripture not only consumed the McGall's and McMaster's time, but more important, it consumed our hearts.

Of course, I could not study the Bible and learn God's Word without being changed. My parents were thrilled to see their prayers answered. Dad was in his element.

Living without God throughout my younger years had broken my heart. Social policy makers in Northern Ireland allude to the poverty of aspiration that affects many communities. Government intervention has helped reduce some forms of material poverty, but a greater poverty lies hidden from public view. A much more insidious form of destruction is the death of hope and constructive desire. I had been its victim, living with the constant wanting something I could not have, and when it ran away from me faster than I could run, I just gave up chasing it. James's observation about the flesh is fitting:

> You covet but you cannot get what you want, so you quarrel and fight. You do not have because you do not ask God. When you ask, you do not receive, because you ask with wrong motives, that you may spend what

you get on your pleasures.

James 4:2–3

I had wanted what others possessed and felt cheated when I hadn't received it. And when that happened, a war raged in my heart. My motives had been all wrong. I was envious of others' success and jealous of their happiness. Like Adam and Eve, I wanted to blame others for what I had lost. If it wasn't the teacher in the classroom who had stolen my confidence, it was the Catholics on the streets who were attempting to take away my identity. Whilst James was speaking of those who pursued materialism, the principle is applicable to anything that displaces God. My sin (flesh) had stolen my future, and along with it my hope.

Thank God the day I asked him to change all that he did! Not all at once, because nurturing hope is a life-long journey, but slowly and surely God was forming hope in my life. My parents could see it in my eyes and hear it in my voice. For the very first time I dared to hope. I ventured to believe that my future could be different from my past. But now, God would be responsible for its direction.

Increasingly, when I pulled back the curtain each morning, I welcomed the sunrise. At night I ceased fearing the sunset. No longer was my bedroom a lonely place. Those voices that once whispered heartache in the dark were one by one being silenced.

Of recent I have been thinking about the power of memory. In particular, how we recall previous events. Here, too, the flesh may leave its fingerprints over our memories.

There is only one inspired history, and it is that of the Bible. I am intrigued how God collected so many stories of disappointment, conflict, betrayal, and human heartache and wove them into the story of redemption. This indeed is a work of divine tapestry. It gives painful experiences a place in his divine purposes. It is a sanctified history, set apart from all other histories because it points us to God.

However, when the flesh recalls our broken moments, it often does so by exasperating the hurts of the past. It segregates the painful from the pleasurable. Then it constructs each painful moment, one on top of the other, building a shrine to uncontrollable bitterness, insistent resentment, and terminal pessimism. Unaware of the fingerprints of the flesh, we pay homage to our pain. We blame everyone and everything for our present struggles. The magnitude of how we have been sinned against is often a poisonous memory of the world's brutality. Some wounds run so deep that healing seems almost impossible.

Yet we must remember the backstory that brings hope. A hidden hand not responsible for the pain may assist us in our healing. The journey of recovery is possible when God sanctifies our memories, if not the events themselves. Those memories are baptised into believing that a redemptive story runs throughout our personal histories. Each event, clearly not good in itself, becomes an opportunity to see God's power and grace at work.

When you think of the past, you can choose how to recall it. You can allow the pain to eclipse God's presence, or you can choose to see the redemptive hand of God. I nursed pain for many years until I realised that God used my pain to nurture within me a desire to learn, study, and show myself to be a workman approved by God. It was out of the depths of hate and sectarianism that God planted a love for all mankind, regardless of class, colour, or creed. It was out of the barren emptiness of a hollow life that God filled it with his pleasure, purpose, and presence. The practice of baptism demonstrates cleansing; perhaps it should be applied to our memories too!

Ian McCammon also attended the Friday night Bible studies. He and I became close friends. He, too, was passionate about his faith. He loved God and served him with his whole heart, soul, and mind. His desire to follow his Saviour would eventually lead him into full-time mission service.

Rarely did Ian and I meet without our conversation turning to God. We would often challenge each other by opening the Word at random verses and say, "Tell me what the Bible is saying there, what it means, how I can apply it to my life."

Ian's pursuit of God was contagious. Our meetings together brought infectious laughter, joy in knowing God, and an enthusiasm for personal evangelism. In our most zealous moments we went door-to-door telling people about the love of Jesus. We stood on the streets together and preached. On one rainy Saturday afternoon, Ian was preaching on sin, including that of theft, only to find that someone had stolen his umbrella! The amusement we shared as we walked home in the rain summed up our joy in the Lord. As the years have passed we have drifted apart. But we had the joy of reconnecting recently, and no matter the lapse of time, our love for the Lord remains strong.

Tony and Valerie, Clare and Campbell, and Ian all helped me to develop a huge thirst for Scripture. Considering that I had never really read a book throughout my school years, other than when forced to read in class, my desire to read and study the Bible was quite remarkable.

The first book I read after becoming a Christian was *The Cross and Switchblade* by David Wilkerson, Nicky Cruz's tremendous story of how he exchanged leading one of the most violent gangs in New York City with becoming a servant of Christ. His powerful words inspired me not only to read the Bible but also to read biographies of Christians. At seventeen years of age, I developed a hunger for books.

I wasn't a member of the Presbyterian Church, even though my father was an elder in Second Randalstown. However, I was attending their youth Bible study and found it tremendously helpful. But a big question still remained.

What will I do with my life?

CHAPTER FIVE

Standing on God's Promises for My Future

Clearly, I was never a good student. In fact, I was never even a fair student. Many times my parents were called into the principals' offices to discuss my lack of academic progress. But nothing changed.

One day while attending the government training centre (GTC), I was sent to see the chief as a result of an altercation with one of the instructors. After he dismissed me back to my class, the chief called my father into his office. As I stood at the lathe, I was embarrassed to watch Dad walk through the shop floor to the office block. Ashamed of my behaviour, I averted my father's gaze. Long story short, I never lasted at GTC to the end of the year!

Even though I had become a Christian during this period of my education, a chain of events were unfolding that were practically irreversible. Not only had the early part of the year been marked by poor behaviour, but I had been failing my exams. One instructor had told me it was impossible to fail City and Guilds. He shouldn't have used the word *impossible*. I did get at least one City and Guilds, in fabrication and welding, which was surprising since I couldn't get the lid on my toolbox to close properly. Though supposedly impossible, I failed all the rest.

Therefore, I decided not to finish my time at GTC. Now a Christian, I hoped a second spell at Antrim Technical College might be more productive. I thought that a fresh start would produce better results.

I fared no better this second time around. Once again I was going to fail yet another set of exams. Mum and Dad always knew that I was going to prop up the class, but as long as I stayed out of trouble they were okay with that.

Before my mother and father were called in to see the principal—again—a female teacher brought me down to the principal's office. In front of me she told the principal, "You know, Alistair is below average mental ability."

All the humiliation I had experienced in primary school washed over me. Even as a Christian and feeling good about the changes God was bringing into my life, her words and my memories stung. They haunted me. Even though I was daring to believe I had a future, it was difficult to hold on to that hope against the backdrop of doubt that surrounded me. At times it seemed that only God and my parents believed in me. Every conventional measure of progress was blocked by my human weakness. Beginning in primary school, my repeated failures and subsequent behavioural problems wounded me. I eventually bought into the lie that I was worthless. When the flesh inflicts its wounds, healing takes time. Once I became a Christian and read in the Bible that I was valuable and had a God-given purpose, the battle between continuing to believe the lies I had lived with for so long and replacing the lies with truth became a daily tug-of-war without an obvious winner. If I couldn't make a toolbox or properly spell, what hope of a future did I have?

My mother and father made me sit in the car as they talked to the principal. The day is clearly etched in my memory: a miserable, rainy day. I felt as gloomy as the weather. I watched the droplets roll down the windscreen while pondering my empty future.

When my parents returned to the car, I thought, "I am in for it again. They are just going to off-load the whole way home."

But my parents were strangely silent. Dad could be quite quick-tempered, but he was very quiet that day. To be honest, I would have preferred his shouting at me rather than his silence. We arrived home and just before we got out of the car he spoke to me. Without turning round, he asked, "Alistair, what are you going to do with your future?"

His words stabbed my heart. I had asked God to direct

my future, and whilst my heart now believed that he would, I had little external evidence. It must have been as tough for my parents as it was for me. They had been blessed to see my progress of growing in my Christian walk and learning God's Word over the short time I had been converted. They could see my passion for God, a fuller and happier life. Yet now, once again, I had another set of failed exams. I was dreaming about heaven, but what was I going to do on earth? Had God a plan for me here too? Just where and when would he lead me?

So I earnestly sought God. "Lord, you have got to direct me. If anyone is going to change me, it has to be you. You have got to find for me a way forward. I don't want to be a disappointment to you. I certainly don't want to be a disappointment to my parents any longer."

By then I had a great concern for my parents. They'd had to contend with a lot from me as I was growing up. I didn't want to cause them any more anguish. I pleaded with God that he would lead me forward.

God always answers our prayers, though not always when or how we want or expect. I had to wait almost a year before he answered mine: a call to the ministry. Along with this answer came more questions, the biggest being: What do I do with this call? I didn't know anything about Bible college or what was involved in being a minister.

I belonged to Antrim Elim, so I visited our pastor, Jimmy Ritchie. I loved Jimmy. He was a terrific pastor and a great evangelist in the pulpit. I was almost nineteen years of age, and Jimmy had become somewhat of a mentor to me. I greatly admired the fire in his heart.

I called round to his house and said, "Jimmy, I feel a

call to the ministry but I don't know what it means exactly or what I'm supposed to do."

He leaned forward in his chair. "Alistair, if you feel a call to the ministry, you certainly seem to have some of the gifts necessary to that type of calling. You have a passion for God, you talk to people about Jesus, and you are not frightened to get up and speak when you are given the opportunity. We could pursue this together. Elim Bible College is a real possibility for you."

I shook my head. "I don't have any standard of qualifications."

"Well, they don't actually require any formal education for you to be considered for their diploma course. I am one of their Northern Ireland representatives. If you make a formal application, I and Pastor McCandless will interview you."

My academic circumstances had brought me to the point of exasperation. I could not be any less prepared for college. I was on supplementary benefit, the lowest form of financial aid given by the government to the unemployed. Still living at home and with no prospects of employment, it wasn't hard to see how God had removed my element of choice. After all, I was practically unemployable since I couldn't work with my hands. Jimmy said I needed to think about working with my brain. The memory of the teacher's accusation increased my apprehension, After all, *Alistair has below average mental ability*. Goliath was still wielding his sword in 1982; his taunt was my severe lack of ability. As Satan whispered cynically in my ears, I was too ready to listen.

Though I believed Jimmy was right, I still felt the most

unlikely of candidates for theological study. Fear, apprehension, and self-doubt flooded my anxious mind. At the same time, excitement and a seed of hope planted at my conversion was beginning to germinate. During that time God impressed the words of Hebrews 11:8 on my heart, "By faith, Abraham, when called to go to a place he would later receive as his inheritance, obeyed and went, even though he did not know where he was going." This passage became a source of great challenge but also immense comfort. I might have known where I was going, but I needed to obey God in getting there. Regardless of the fears and doubts that gripped my heart, it came down to a matter of whom I should trust. Did I want to put my trust in my old life¬—a flesh-life imprisoned by fear, loneliness, failure, and a cycle of emptiness—or trust God for a new beginning? I had nothing to lose.

I submitted my application to Elim Bible College, a training centre of the Pentecostal church. My interview was to be held in Ballymena Elim Church. Jimmy borrowed an XR3i to drive me to the church. I was extremely nervous about the interview and Jimmy's driving only added to it. He opened her up on the motorway, and as we were approaching a junction, a car pulled out in front of us. I smelled burnt rubber for days.

Once the interview began, I took a few deep breaths and answered the questions as honestly as I could. I had to wait a few weeks for the response. I remember very little about that wait, or, indeed, how I felt. Disappointment had been my constant companion, so I avoided thinking too far into the future. A few weeks later I received an acceptance letter inviting me on to Elim Bible College's diploma course. I was hoping that this change of direction would lead to a successful conclusion.

Perhaps my parents, my pastor, my friends, and especially I would be happy at last!

If only life were that simple.

CHAPTER SIX

Standing out as A Prankster

Elim Bible College provided a sense of community. I lived on campus along with the other students, further solidifying camaraderie between us all.

Still in my theological and Christian infancy, I was a pain in the neck to my professors and fellow students during my first year. Looking back, I cringe at my arrogance I had as a young Christian. The patience the lecturers and students possessed was unbelievable.

In the first year I managed to get myself expelled, along with six other culprits, over a complete misunderstanding. Considering what my parents had been through with me already, you can imagine how they felt when I telephoned them with the news!

Near the end of my freshman year, our workload was beginning to lighten. And, as you might expect, several of us played pranks and entered into mischief.

One particular Welsh guy always wore a cravat. One day, a few of us guys challenged him: "Listen, if we beat you in three arm wrestles, can we dump you in the bath?" I'm not sure why, but he accepted. We picked three of the strongest-looking guys who would arm wrestle this young man (who wore a cravat!).

We managed to beat him and even gave him a pair of swimming trunks to minimise his distress. He changed into the trunks and then we chased him along the top floor corridor of our dorm. We managed to grab him, but the ice-cold water of the bath made him reconsider complying with the terms of our agreement. Consequently, he tried grabbing the door frame to keep from being dunked into the water. I seized a broken chair leg that was lying close by and whacked the door quite close to his fingers without hurting him to get him to loosen his grasp (coming from Northern Ireland, my aim was good). We dumped our victim into the bath and then quickly disappeared.

After the incident, one of my partners in pranks and I made our way along the bottom corridor and out into the car park just outside the Brewster Wing. It was then we noticed the principal marching along the passageway.

The principal, Rev. Eldin Corsie, used to be in The Black Watch, an infantry battalion of the Regiment of Scotland and was a force to be reckoned with. With his sleeves rolled up and his collar open, he was on the warpath. My friend and I looked at each other and said in unison, "Somebody is in trouble."

He fairly marched towards us before shouting at the top of his voice: "Were you two involved?"

Because I was the one who spoke all the time, I said, "Involved in what?"

He pointed his sharp razor-like finger at me. "Don't act innocent with me! Were you involved?"

"Involved in what?" I repeated.

"The bathroom!"

My friend and I answered, "Yeah."

"You're out!" His voice thundered. "Pack your bags. You are going home. You're finished at Elim Bible College."

I was stunned, as was my colleague. We turned and shuffled back up to our rooms where the six of us gathered. We wondered what we were going to do, hardly believing we had been kicked out of Bible college. We discussed this for about an hour. I went downstairs to the main house to phone my parents. I was nervous, frustrated, and confused. It rang for a few seconds and then I heard a quiet, "Hello."

After a few seconds of silence, I said, "I have been put out of Elim Bible College."

"What do you mean 'put out'?" my parents said.

"I have actually been expelled." I explained about the prank. "It upset the principal, so he expelled us."

I swallowed hard at the silence on the other end of the

phone. I don't think they knew what to make of it—of me. Then I said: "Listen, I will go pack my bags. If something changes, I will let you know." We hung up and I went upstairs to pack.

While I was on the phone, the other guys went to see the Dean of Students, Mr. Hunt. Because he wanted to see all six of us, I ended up in his office too. Mr. Hunt was also the principal's brother-in-law. We hoped this familial relationship would allow us to know why the principal had gotten so angry with us over a seemingly innocent prank.

After explaining the situation to Mr. Hunt, he said, "You need to go and see Rev. Corsie again, that is, if you want to be reinstated."

I stepped forward. "I am not doing it, because he has just been bawling and shouting." I turned on my heels and marched back to my room to continue to pack. Within the hour, some of the guys came into the dorm laughing.

"What are you laughing at?" I said.

"Rev. Corsie just took us to the bathroom to complain about the mess. He said 'There is water everywhere. You boys don't even belong to the Main Block. You live in the Brewster wing. Why have you flooded this bathroom?' We let him go on for five minutes before we said, 'That wasn't the bath we put him into; it was the other one, upstairs.' Unhappy with that, he then shouted at us for being up here in the first place."

Upon reflection, Rev. Corsie decided his initial response and verdict was unnecessary and reversed himself. Everyone made their way down to the canteen for tea.

I was never officially reinstated as I was never part of those discussions, but I presume I was allowed to return because I graduated two years later!

I tell this story because Eldin Corsie was one of the most influential men in my life at that stage of my Christian walk. (I have since forgiven him for throwing me out.)

My theological outlook at this point had shifted to Reformed, so I chose not to pursue the Elim ministry. Yet Eldin was a man of great integrity and character who demonstrated a patience I am still trying to emulate. Mr. Hunt, the Dean of Students, also showed impeccable grace towards this outspoken Irishman. I was an impetuous young Christian whose brashness permeated every facet of my character.

During my first year at Elim, I was adamantly opposed to women preaching and wanted my opposition to be fully realised. On one memorable occasion, a lady was to present her sermon to the homiletics class. The students and professors would evaluate not only the content of the sermons but also the presentation.

I sat at the back of the room and waited for her to get up to speak. As she did, I walked from the back of the class, navigated past her out the door, and closed the door behind me with a firm click. The defender of the faith had left the building. I would not sit under a woman who was preaching that day, or any day for that matter.

It wasn't long before I was summoned to the dean's office to give an account of my actions. I had offended this particular woman, and my actions had caused considerable pain and grievance. After a protracted discussion with the dean, perhaps more in hope than expectation, he handed me a book written by J. C. Ryle entitled *Knots Untied*.

Mr. Hunt said, "Alistair, you are a young lad full of conviction, and I respect that. But you must learn to channel your convictions constructively. It's okay to have passion and conviction, but you needn't upset the world around you in seeking to express them. You must understand the context; it wasn't appropriate to make a protest in the way you did. It certainly hasn't furthered your cause, and it didn't inspire this lady to feel any better about the beliefs you hold."

I duly noted his grace and wisdom. And whilst it took many more years for me to develop it as a template to live by, he had, at least, planted seeds that would produce a harvest in years to come. It helped to shape and mould my beliefs and practices today. I seek to conduct ministry in a much more tolerant manner, even though I still hold to some of my early convictions. I have learned to be aware of whom I'm working with, their background, and their beliefs and convictions.

Why do so many Christians feel they have the right to offend others? I have learned that the gospel is offensive enough without allowing the deficient and sinful components of my personality to be a stumbling block to its reception by unbelievers. How many people have been alienated from God, not by what was said, but by the way it was said?

Mr. Hunt and Rev. Corsie, both godly men, gave me a legacy that was to bear fruit many years later. Unfortunately, they never got to see the benefits of their contributions in my life, but I am sure one day God will show them the fruits of their labour.

As I look back over the years, I am convinced now that my flesh won more battles than I care to realise. At times, my ego masqueraded as conviction was demonstrated in my refusal to lose an argument. Those debates were less about protecting truth and more about establishing credibility. That's the problem with human brokenness, it can follow you like a shadow. I had been humiliated at school through lack of knowledge, but now that I felt more comfortable and proficient in my knowledge, I did not mind whom I hurt in order to prove my newfound capabilities. But over time the Spirit gradually gained control through genuine repentance, saturation in the Word of God, and a willingness to engage with the Holy Spirit. The flesh, albeit reluctantly, began to lose its grip. However, wars within are one thing, but our collective weakness is saturated with brokenness.

The war against the flesh began in the garden of Eden. It is the fruit of disobedience. God had given specific instructions that Adam and Eve were not to eat of the Tree of the Knowledge of Good and Evil. We can only speculate as to why God planted the tree, but what is undeniable is that good and evil existed prior to this tree's existence. Satan had already been cast out of heaven, taking with him a third of the angelic kingdom. Knowledge of good and evil permeated the universe, and those excluded from heaven possessed the flawed capacity to make judgements. Satan himself accused Job of serving God with wrong motives. As such, it revealed his inclination to make distorted judgements regarding a person's character and motivations.

This knowledge of good and evil is dangerous when a person is disorientated from God. Working now with limited knowledge and tainted motivations, we fracture relationships, foster cynicism, and embrace the condemnation of others. We supplant the Lord as judge, for he alone can make a flawless judgment of a person's heart.

Whilst Adam and Eve had known only the good, they did not judge each other, or accuse God of any impropriety. Satan, on the other hand, has a memory of the good but is incapable of performing it. Aware of his evil intent, Satan became vulnerable to its control and dominance. The evil he embodies is fuelled by his pride and arrogance. While innocent of evil, Adam and Eve remained in a perfect bond with God and each other. However, since the fall, and for the first time, they made judgements of each other. In this now flesh-orientated state, they blamed each other for their sin. They had taken upon themselves the sole right of judging others. Adam sought to establish his own innocence by directing God's attentions to the imperfections of Eve. Eve followed in his footsteps and accused the devil. With the entrance of sin into the world, humanity has continued the blame game.

In this fallen state, the knowledge of good and evil appeals to our imperfections. We all too ready to assume God's sole position by evaluating the actions of others. But we don't stop there. We also condemn others for their actions. We manifest the good and become proud; we see our own evil and condemn ourselves. We witness the sins of others and join the chorus of disapproval. We align ourselves with God's greatest enemy, Satan, and too quickly become the accuser of the brethren. We have uprooted the Tree of Knowledge of Good and Evil from the garden and carry it with us every day. Our knowledge of both good and evil does not comfort us or rightly accuse us. Satan had suggested that Adam and Eve would be like God if they ate from such a tree, but the truth is, they became more like the devil himself—and so went all of humanity. We possess a memory of the good, but in a flesh-orientated life we are controlled by evil and dominated by its influences.

However, this battle is not without victory. The possibility of defeating the flesh is now within our grasp. Jesus said to Nicodemus, "You must be born from above," and that's exactly what happens at conversion. At the point of repentance of sin, our lives are reorientated towards God. In this new orientation, we have new desires. We gladly receive his teaching and are enthusiastic to fulfil his commands. Most of all, we desire to be willing disciples. Yet, we soon become aware that sheer willpower or effort will not achieve such objectives. We need something or, more accurately, Someone to help us fulfil these divine and noble objectives.

Jesus declared that his finished work on the cross had atoned for sin, removing its penalty, breaking its power, and promising one day the removal of its presence altogether. Yet in order to progress that reality, he promised the Holy Spirit to be present in our lives. On the day of Pentecost, his anticipated arrival came, and the once inept, easily confused, and seriously impoverished disciples experienced a new power. Now controlled by the Holy Spirit, their transformation embraced a new boldness, holiness, and divine focus that had previously evaded them. What was true for them can now be a reality for us. In Romans 8:5–8, Paul's directive is clear: we are no longer controlled by the flesh, even though we may still be influenced by it.

> Those who live according to the flesh have their minds

> set on what the flesh desires; but those who live in accordance with the Spirit have their minds set on what the Spirit desires. The mind governed by the flesh is death, but the mind governed by the Spirit is life and peace. The mind governed by the flesh is hostile to God; it does not submit to God's law, nor can it do so. Those who are in the realm of the flesh cannot please God.

The Bible gives us a significant rebuke. We must have our minds set on Christ, not on the old life disorientated by sin. When no change of behaviour is discernible, we lack assurance of salvation. The Bible presumes a change of conduct as evidence of our conversation. Yet it takes time for the mind of Christ to be formed in us, and the process of being changed from one degree of glory to the next assumes a progression towards God's ideal for our lives. Without the power of the Holy Spirit, such a journey would be rendered impossible, and we could neither resist the Enemy nor avoid being conformed to the pattern of this world. Indeed, it is the pattern of this world that many of us struggle with, and the very reason we struggle with it is because we have never overcome the flesh. When you have overcome your flesh, then you're ready to take on the world.

PART TWO: THE WORLD

You adulterous people, don't you know that friendship with the world means enmity against God? Therefore, anyone who chooses to be a friend of the world becomes an enemy of God.

James 4:4

For everything in the world—the lust of the flesh, the lust of the eyes, and the pride of life—comes not from the Father but from the world.

1 John 2:16

As a teenager I thought I was the only one who had broken desires, feelings, and impulses. The nights of dark thoughts, lonely moments, and dying aspirations had become part of my daily ritual. As I was being changed by God's grace, I was tempted to forget how life had felt without God. I wanted heaven long before it would arrive. The church became my dwelling place. I felt good behind the safety of its walls. With different friends, new songs, and more wholesome desires, it had become my virtual garden of Eden.

Well, it would have been, until I found out that Christians sin too! Nevertheless, they appeared to sin less than non-Christians, and that was a good thing. My journey of personal restoration took me to a place full of Christians, called Bible college, and the steep learning curve of how to grow in God's grace, but it also took me back into the world where I would have the pleasure of witnessing God's grace at work.

The irony of my discovery was that the very same dark thoughts, lonely moments, and dying aspirations where shared by others. At last my broken life made sense. With memories of my own brokenness, I could readily identify with a world shattered by sin. If the good news could find me, I was convinced that it could find them too.

For God so loved the world that he gave his one and only Son, that whoever believes in him shall not perish but have eternal life.

John 3:16

"I have told you these things, so that in me you may have peace. In this world you will have trouble. But take heart! I have overcome the world.

John 16:33

CHAPTER SEVEN

Standing on the Grace of Forgiveness

A Day of Prayer had been scheduled at Elim Bible College, with Clive Calver, the Director of the Evangelical Alliance, as the invited speaker. Before we knew of this event, four of us students had planned to go to Wimbledon to see John

McEnroe and Jimmy Connors.

The morning of the Day of Prayer and before we were to set off for Wimbledon, my three friends and I got together and had a theological discussion as to whether we should go to Wimbledon or attend the Day of Prayer. We decided to go to the tennis match, reasoning that we can pray every day of the week, but we'd have the opportunity to watch McEnroe and Connors play only once in our lifetime.

My standing at Elim Bible College was tenuous enough, as I had already been expelled that year. Nevertheless, on the grassy slopes of Wimbledon we enjoyed our strawberries and cream. We had queued for hours, and now stood in the free standing area, packed like sardines in a tin. I remember looking at the grass in amazement. It was perfect, almost like someone had cut it with scissors. The sunlight danced off every polished surface, and the sound of each tennis rally produced a hypnotic effect.

We returned home from London that night after a fantastic day of viewing tennis matches and watching McEnroe throwing tantrums. It was a wonderful experience.

Upon returning to our dorm, a distressed student met us at the door. He informed us that the principal had put letters in our "pigeon hole." I presumed it wasn't a thank-you card. We sheepishly went in search of the letters, but to our relief, the pigeon holes were empty. Returning to our colleague we said, "You are having us on. There are no letters there. We are not in trouble at all."

"No, you are in trouble. Your absence was noted, and he placed those letters in your pigeon hole at lunchtime," he said.

"Well, they are not there now," I said.

I learned later that the principal, Eldin Corsie, had removed the letters after the evening service. That evening Clive Calver had spoken about the need to forgive others. In contemplating the theme, the principal had a change of heart. If he had not, I might have had a change of vocation.

James 4:4 declares that friendship with the world puts us at enmity with God. Perhaps Eldin had felt hurt, offended, and disappointed with my flagrant disregard of his authority as principal. His intended efforts of providing spiritual support and enabling discipleship had been rejected. Instead of raising my hands in prayer, I had joined my hands together in the applause of mere mortals. Again in chapter four, James moves his attention away from the battle within each one of us to what we collectively battle together.

Echoing the words of Hosea 3:1, "The lord said to me, 'Go, show your love to your wife again, though she is loved by another man and is an adulteress. Love her as the lord loves the Israelites, though they turn to other gods and love the sacred raisin cakes.'" Maybe Eldin felt that I had chosen other things above God, perhaps he was even right. Nevertheless, rather than nurse his wounds and rationalise his response, he was willing to forgive. To love as the Lord loves requires tremendous grace. As James 4:6 states, "But he gives us more grace. That is why Scripture says: 'God opposes the proud but shows favor to the humble.'" James recognised his audience's pride had led to quarrels and division. They had not been prepared to love as God did. In fact, they stood defiant, unwilling to be filled with the Spirit and to live as a people of grace and humility.

Eldin could have joined a chorus of criticism against my actions, but he chose not to. Rather, his change of heart was not manmade but God inspired. Acting like his Father in heaven, Eldin showed forgiveness to one who had erred.

Is God tugging at your heart as you read this? Who needs to be the recipient of your humility? Refuse to nurse your hurts and instead show love. Stretch out the hand of forgiveness and be reconciled.

Clive Calver doesn't know that I am a graduate of Elim Bible College and a minister of the Presbyterian church in Ireland. But both of these accomplishments are due in no small part to his sermon and God's timely intervention. The world may deem it as a coincidence or a chance encounter with Lady Luck. The sceptics will postulate that my reflections are a human construct to give life meaning and purpose. Yet friendship with God places us at enmity with the world. Eldin chose not to act like the world, and today I consciously choose not to think like it either. As I reflect on my journey, I detect the guiding hand of God. He has taught me many things, often through my mistakes. But if we believe in the sovereignty and providence of God, then all our actions are connected with his divine purposes. One action can have many unforeseen consequences. Does anyone truly know the blessings or fruit of his or her ministry? That is why we keep going. Clive was oblivious to the impact of his sermon, and Eldin is unaware of the lives that have been touched as a result of his act of grace, forgiveness, and humility. I was shown forgiveness, and I have shown that same forgiveness to others. It started with one man's obedience and another man's humility. I was blessed as a result and others have been blessed as a consequence. Thank God, the virtuous circle continues to this day.

CHAPTER EIGHT

Standing with God Through Heartache

A far less positive memory whilst attending Elim Bible College was failing my first theological assignment. I collected my essay from the professor's office and sheepishly opened the front cover to learn my mark: 35 percent. I was speechless, which cannot be said of the examiner, who, in a rather nonchalant tone, remarked, "Alistair, you are only ever going to be mediocre in terms of your academic progress." The shadows of the past hung low over me. Would its darkness follow me everywhere? Would I ever feel the warmth of sunshine on my accomplishments?

I remember praying, "Lord, why would you call me here to humiliate me with failure? At every turn, my confidence is shattered by setbacks and disappointments. If I am going to get through this, you will have to rescue me."

I visited Julian Ward, who was also the Academic Director at the college. He looked at my essay, noted my anaemic grade, and said, "Alistair, you are enrolled for the Cambridge Certificate in Religious Studies and the Elim Bible College Diploma. I don't think you will be able to do the Cambridge qualification. Would you not consider coming off that programme and just doing the internal exams? After all, you are here as a ministry student."

I pled with him. "Please, let me do this. With God's help I think I can complete it."

After a long, thoughtful pause, very reluctantly Julian said, "Okay. If you feel strongly enough, who am I to stand in your way?"

Three years later, in 1986, I graduated not only with a distinction in the Elim Bible College Diploma but also with the Cambridge Certificate in Religious Studies. It was a proud day for both my parents as they travelled across the Irish Sea to England to watch their son graduate. I am sure some of the faculty presumed it to be a miracle as well. A broken world had battered my confidence, but God was gradually restoring it.

The broken systems of this world, and how they measure success, had deemed me a failure. Thank God that when the world lost faith in me God refused to. That same God inspired others to hope, believing in me as well. In faith, when all the evidence pointed to the contrary, they prayed and believed God had a purpose for my life. I was learning the value of Proverbs 3:5–6: "Trust in the Lord with all your heart and lean not on your own understanding; in all your ways submit to him, and he will make your paths straight." The journey of submitting to God is a long and difficult road to travel. The pathway through a maze is not hard to determine from an elevated vantage point, but it sure is challenging when surrounded by hedges that block the view. The walk of faith is required when life seems confusing and tough. However, submitting to God when the way ahead seems unclear is at least one indication that both the flesh and the world are relinquishing their grip on one's life, thoughts, and heart.

As my theological position had altered from Pentecostal to Reformed, I could not sign the Pentecostal church's statement of faith, rendering my application to the Pentecostal ministry impossible. So not wishing to go into full-time ministry, I followed in my father's footsteps and entered the workforce in the insurance industry.

Whilst I appreciated those jobs, I could never settle. I knew this was not what my life's work was to be so I continued to search as to what God wanted me to do. Eventually, I went back for a part-time degree at Queen's University Belfast from 1988–89 for my Bachelor of Arts degree in General Studies. This included an introductory module in Philosophy and Literature, which I passed.

I then applied to Queen's, but I didn't possess O-Level English; therefore, the university was reluctant to process my application.

God used a sceptic of Christianity to fight in my corner. He was one of the most colourful lecturers I have ever met. An English tutor and a little eccentric, he had the skill of drawing his students into learning then sending them away wanting to know more. He knew I was finding it difficult to make a competent application to the university. He wrote a personal letter to the Admissions Department at Queens University, guaranteeing that I would pass the course. He agreed to stand over my work and make sure that happened, even though I would be enrolled in a different discipline taught by a different department. Encouragement can often come from the most unlikely sources, and God used this man to further his purposes in my life.

Just months before I was accepted into Queens was a difficult time for me, as my mother became very ill with breast cancer. I so desperately wanted God to heal her. Throughout the years she had been a tower of strength to me, believing in me even when I didn't believe in myself. The previous year, 1988, just after receiving her diagnosis, my father had come into the office in Ballymena where I worked to tell me that my mother was ill. That was the first time I had ever seen my father cry. He had been in the RAF, a culture that insists that men don't cry. To see him broken was devastating. I remember thinking that my parents were meant to cry and worry about me, not the other way around. I felt too young to assume that role for them.

Dad asked me to go out to the car where my Mother was sitting and pretend as if nothing was amiss. The old saying "life must go on" is a stoic response, but life never just goes on. It changes. But we are encouraged to take one day at

a time, and that's all we could do.
I carried on with my Foundation Module in Philosophy and Literature and passed it. During that time, my mum was diagnosed with secondary cancer of the liver. Her prognosis was poor. She was discharged from Belvoir Park Hospital and brought home.

We had moved into temporary accommodation on the Coolsythe Road. In a moment of desperation, I prayed to God, "Lord, what is going to happen to my mother?" God spoke to me from John 17:11. Much of the passage was a blur until I read the following verse, "Father, I want those you have given me to be with me where I am" (CSB). God moved my spirit to read John chapter 17 for a very specific reason. He drew my heart and my mind to that verse, which convinced me that my mother would not survive the cancer. It could not have been clearer. God had spoken to me quite distinctly that she would not survive long.

God had imprinted this in my heart because I needed to know what was to be, and he needed to reassure me that his wish for my mother was greater than my earthly desire to retain her. Her work on earth was done. She had prayed for me and asked that God would take me into ministry. Though she would not live so see that, like the heroes of the faith in Hebrews 11, she lived in anticipation that God would keep his promise. I was content that God was taking her to a better place and that her prayers had finally been answered.

I never spoke to my Father about this because I wanted him to enjoy their remaining days. They never talked about her illness until towards the end. They simply believed that all of their days, just like the family, were in his hands.

When people love each other, why lament what God removes? Rather, be grateful that he gave you this relationship in the first place.

At the time of Mum's death, I learned how precious the family of God could be. The Rev Jack Kelly demonstrated that great teachers could also be wonderful pastors. Fred and Florence were typical of many in 2nd Randalstown, who wrapped us in their arms of love providing invaluable support. Lessons in tenderness never forgotten.

Shortly after Mum's death, I received a letter of confirmation by the university. My place had been secured. Of course, Dad knew my intentions to train for the ministry, but after Mum's death, he shared a story that was to change my perception of hope, vision, and faith, which I hold to this very day.

"Alistair, when you were going through those very difficult years, your mum used to lock herself in the bathroom. I could hear her sobbing. She was in floods of tears because her heart was broken by what was happening in your life. I remember one particular evening when she came down from the bathroom into the living room. She stood beside me and said, 'Meredith, it is going to be okay.'

"I asked, 'Why, May? Why is it going to be okay?'

"She replied, 'I have prayed for Alistair, and I have said, "Lord, I don't just want you to save Alistair, I want you to take him into full-time ministry. I don't want him to do anything else but to walk with you and to serve you for the rest of his life." And God is going to do it.'"

Mum had offered her prayer of faith before my conversation, and God had given her the reassurance without any signs of immediate fulfilment or hope. She had a deep unwavering conviction that God had spoken and that he would keep his word. As the night air chilled the skies, hope had flooded into her heart that he not only would save me but also call me into full-time Christian service. Though she saw and rejoiced in my salvation, Mum died before I could tell her that I was going to progress towards the Presbyterian ministry. But perhaps she didn't need to see it. It was good enough that God had promised it. Knowing that Mum believed God would bring me to him has helped me to believe this same thing for other parents whose children seem to have turned their backs on the one Person who is the answer to their every need. We should never give up hope on a wayward child, regardless of what he or she may put us through.

Over the years I have learned how sweet the hope of resurrection is. A world without God sees death as futile, pointless, a decomposition of matter. Not so for the believer. We join in a chorus of approval with the apostle Paul when he writes, "Brothers and sisters, we do not want you to be uninformed about those who sleep in death, so that you do not grieve like the rest of mankind, who have no hope" (1 Thess. 4:13). Mankind may bury their hearts in despair. Without hope we return to earth, ashes, and dust. But for the church, hope springs eternal. One day we will see Jesus face-to-face and embrace all those who loved Jesus to the end.

CHAPTER NINE

Standing with New Perspectives

It was only a matter of weeks after my mother's funeral that I entered Queen's University Belfast (1989). She would have been so pleased. I am sure she would have thought back to that day I cried at the prospect of going to primary school. How she would have rejoiced at witnessing my transformation: the heartache of humiliation; paralysing fear; and a crushed spirit replaced with laughter, intrigue, and discovery! In short, I had an absolute ball at Queen's.

I started off doing the single honours degree in Social Anthropology. I was the only Christian in the class, or at least the only visible Christian witness. I got absolutely hammered by some of the lecturers for what I believed about the Christian faith, but rather than weaken my faith or cause me to walk away from it, the interaction, which I thoroughly enjoyed, served to strengthen and even sharpen my faith. It was all a process of learning.

I actually thrived in this environment, and I graduated in 1992 with a 2:1 in Social Anthropology. Subsequently, I completed a Bachelor of Divinity degree in 1995 with a 2:1 classification. I had also managed to secure a few scholarship prizes in my final year.

As I walked along the platform to receive my first degree, my father and wife sat in the balcony. Hazel and I had met at Elim Bible College and had married in August 1991. She told me later that day that Dad had virtually been impossible to tolerate. He had almost unbridled pride. When he thought about all that I had been through and my academic failures, my graduation meant more to him that I could ever appreciate.

Returning to my seat after receiving my award, I was overwhelmed by a profound moment of disappointment. I thought, "Is this it? Is this what getting a degree feels like?" I had imagined that walking across the platform would have resolved my feeling of inadequacy. I had believed that decades of failure would have been dissolved in a moment of academic achievement. How sadly mistaken I had been. But God did not leave me to wallow in this heightened moment of despondency. He intervened with a direct, uncompromising, and hard-hitting question: "Who are you trying to impress? You are studying in obedience to me, but in your brokenness you are striving for recognition. You are attempting to prove to others that their perception of you is wrong."

The teacher who had lifted me by the scruff of the neck had left his fingerprints on my soul for decades. In the intervening years, I had found the Light of the World. However, when I was described as below average mentally, someone had snuffed that light. Trapped in my memories and destructively motivated by them, I had believed that a parchment that confirmed my degree would liberate me. But now, even my idol mocked me as it tumbled.

It is true that my last three years had been filled with laughter, intrigue, and discovery, but the last discovery was a brutal one: worldly success at best is short-lived, and at worst is empty. The satisfaction I thought success would bring evaded me. The recognition I sought as a result revealed my tarnished motivations. It was yet another attempt by God to expose idols all too readily embraced in Western culture, namely, education. We applaud the status that educational qualifications bring. We mount our achievements on walls, parade our qualifications on platforms, pulpits, and social media. This in itself may not be wrong, but when it encourages us to applaud ourselves and think of ourselves more highly than we ought, then it is wrong. Particularly when that celebration is set within the context of competitiveness, individualism, and intellectual snobbery. If I am being brutally honest, maybe I was applauding myself more loudly than my well-wishers, and God in his gentle grace was letting me hear its hollow ring.

It was then that God began his gentle process of recovery and healing. He soothed me with words impressed upon my heart. "You don't have to prove anything to anyone. I brought you here, I have given you the tools to do this job, and you have done it well."

Over the years God has deepened that impression and fuelled my desire to enjoy the beauty of truthful knowledge. Learning and knowledge must always be our servant and never our master. We must learn so that others may benefit from our knowledge. We must never use our knowledge as a tool for self-promotion.

Learn so that idols can be broken and not created. If you are learning about the development, structure, and function of society, then use that knowledge to provide equality, shared resources, and mechanisms to protect the vulnerable. Many subject areas uncover idols: power, materialism, individualism, and prejudice are but a few. A constructive application of that knowledge is designed to help others, not foster our careers and nurture our egos. When we advance our status, increase our incomes, and differentiate ourselves from others, we have then harvested a corrupted fruit from the Tree of Knowledge of Good and Evil. However, all knowledge that comes under the redemptive power of God has the power to set people free.

Acquire knowledge to liberate others politically, socially, morally, and spiritually. Knowledge is not always about certainty. Within evangelicalism, we want to remain true to tenets of faith that unite us —and unashamedly so—

but that does not mean we are certain over secondary issues, like water baptism, the gifts of the Spirit, etc. To adopt this position helps us avoid arrogance. Learning is a lifelong process. Learn and keep learning, not to win arguments, but to produce Christ-like disciples. The humblest student finds great pleasure in the journey towards knowledge, not simply the possession of it. I still struggle with the complexities of life. My intellectual limitations are all too apparent. Frequently I meet people who struggle with doubts, uncertain as to how to make sense of their personal world. I long to be invited into their world so that we can journey together. The knowledge we acquire isn't just for personal benefit but for the greater good of others. My educational journey enabled me to recognise that it's not about academic qualifications but how the use of truthful knowledge can liberate others.

However, before we can use our knowledge to liberate others, we must be liberated ourselves. The more we read, understand, and accumulate that sort of knowledge, the more we can communicate with people from various backgrounds and, hopefully, introduce them to God. After all, our Great Commission must also become our greatest passion, which is to go and make disciples of all nations.

CHAPTER TEN

Standing in My First Pulpit

My father never got to see my ordination, as he passed away in 1993, just four years after Mum. Hazel and I had married in August 1991. As we were both students, we were living with Dad. It was a cold night in January. After graduating from Queen's University Belfast, I was completing my first set of exams at Union Theological College. Dad had been ill the night before, but it didn't appear to be serious. Because we had finished our last exam of the winter term, the lads wanted to go for coffee and unwind. Knowing that my dad had been poorly, I called home to make sure that everything was okay. The telephone line was engaged (back in the day of land lines), and I presumed he was fine, so I went for a quick coffee.

But when I returned home, I found Dad was very ill. Hazel was training to be a nurse at Whiteabbey Hospital, so when she came home later that evening, she quickly assessed that Dad was deteriorating rapidly. We immediately called the doctor. When he arrived, he determined that Dad required an injection of a particular drug, but he had none with him. He went back to the health centre to retrieve the medicine and also called the ambulance. He returned about ten minutes later. I stood at the gate waiting for the ambulance to arrive while the doctor attended my dad. A few moments later, he made his way downstairs and out to me at the gate. I knew by his expression that my father had passed away.

My brother arrived what seemed like moments later. I couldn't even speak to him but only shook my head. I knew how upset Hazel would be with Dad's passing, as she had loved him dearly. We are a close family, and this loss hurt.

That night, still in my twenties, I had lost both parents. I felt like a child again.

Afterwards, in conversation with my family, I learned that Dad had tried to ring for help and had not replaced the telephone receiver properly. It was then I had called home to check on him and got the busy signal. While my brother, Hazel, and I were reminiscing, I recalled as a child standing on the steps of the portakabin at Finaghy Primary School, trying to work out what age I would be in the year 2000: thirty-six. I had believed then that I would be old enough, perhaps even brave enough, to lose my parents. But that night I admitted that I wasn't old enough; no one is ever old enough to lose one's parents. It was tough, and I miss both of my parents more today than I did all those nights ago.

Hazel had stayed by Dad's side during his remaining minutes on earth. In those final few moments when they were waiting for the ambulance to arrive, Hazel said to Dad, "Don't worry."

"I'm not," he answered.

And he wasn't. Dad missed Mum. After she had gone, he tried to fill his life with ponies and visits to friends, but his life had never been the same. Outside of his great love for Jesus, he had a special love for her.

Faced with making Dad's final arrangements, we were surprised to learn that he had taken care of everything, including all the paperwork that would allow us to plan his funeral and begin the process of probate. It was as if he knew his time was short.

Of this I am certain: both of my parents left me a legacy that has become part of my ministry today. My only sorrow is that they are not here to share in it.

When I could see no future for myself, and even when they could see none for me, Mum and Dad believed that God had plans for me. That's how they lived. Mum had sacrificed in order to bring God's plans for me to fruition. She had gone to work and gone without to make sure my fees were paid. She kept a little black savings book in which only £6 was left after all my schooling fees had been paid. Along with my father, she worked hard to enable me to achieve what I did. I owe them a great deal. Clearly, they were a tremendous influence on my life.

As I began my student assistantship in First Ballymena Presbyterian in 1995, I thought of my parents. How pleased they would have been to see God's plan for my life unfold.

As a young family, Hazel, Hannah (our newborn daughter), and I were taken into the hearts of the congregation of First Ballymena. They showed understanding, kindness, and support in every way possible. Hazel and I absolutely loved the congregation, with our ministry being directed towards young people. The congregation enabled us to explore ministry in creative and unconventional ways.

We were blessed to see the average attendance at youth fellowship increase from eleven to forty-five. The church provided a budget that allowed us to bring in people with amazing gifts. Talented acts like Rodd and Marco joined us from Scotland. (Rodd played Spencer in the children's series *Balamory*.) Steve Legg, an escapologist, mesmerised the young people. In record time he wriggled free from his straight jacket. The parallel was not lost, as young people were challenged to find their freedom in Christ. Rob Lacey, who wrote *The Street Bible*, performed a play entitled *People Like Us*. You could hear a pin drop as young people were encouraged to drop the masks of pretence and discover themselves as God's unique creation. Jonny Gillet, a mime artist who had trained under Marcel Marceau, made a deep impression on their hearts. Stunt rider Paul Sinclair came from Scotland and brought his motorbike. He performed a number of stunts at a local high school and in the church car park. His sense of humour and power of communication endeared himself to all who attended. These were fantastic days filled with energy, excitement, and the presence of God.

Our daughter, Hannah, started to attend Youth Fellowship from only three weeks of age. Hazel brought her down in her little car seat. We poured out our lives into these young people. We loved them and wanted them to experience God's unconditional love. Only then would they build lives worth living.

Doing good youth work requires good listening skills, patience, empathy, and hard work. It calls upon the ability to encourage young people when they get it right and challenge them when they get it wrong. But the most important attitude of all is to continue to love them regardless of what they do or become.

Whenever we brought in Christian artists to put on a mission, we made sure that it was excellent in both its preparation and presentation. God requires our best, and we must work hard to facilitate that. We put together our own youth programme that involved whole-hearted commitment by everyone. I could not have achieved this without Hazel's unstinting support. Hazel and I had no grandparents to call on for help with our baby daughter, for by then, my mum and dad had died and Hazel's parents lived in England. The congregation was fantastic in its support, yet I had to rely on Hazel's sense of calling as we both poured our lives into the work.

I believed then, and still do, that it is essential for youth workers/performers to take ownership of their ministries. I wanted our youth leaders to think prayerfully, creatively, and passionately about what they presented to young people. Those leaders were all students in Belfast, so each week I made a ninety-mile round-trip to discuss the programme with them. Often on Sunday afternoon, it would take a few hours to set up the hall for our multi-media presentation. Rarely did these young people complain, for they had learned the value of effort. Our missions would often take a full week in decorating the hall to make visitors feel welcome and comfortable. Was it worth it? Absolutely! Over the years we had the joy of leading young people to faith and watching them grow into present-day disciples. Some today are serving God as elders in the same church, so, yes, every minute of preparation was worth it.

My advice to every aspiring youth worker is this: If your ministry with youth is worth doing, then for God's honour make sure it is done right. There are no shortcuts to blessing. Do not engage in frenetic activity. Not only does this dishonour God, but, sadly, you will burn out. You don't have to impress others or convince your boss that you work hard. But you do have to work at being a disciple of Christ. Take time to be refreshed and shaped by him. You must spend a few hours each week letting God shape, mould, and inspire you. If not, you will be shaped by the broken world and expectations of others around you. Only when you are spiritually healthy can you promote the health of others.

Don't lament what God is doing elsewhere; rather, celebrate what he is doing right where he has placed you. Convince young people that God wants the best of our talents and not the leftovers of our week. Walking with God is not like cramming for an exam. It takes consistency and daily preparation to enjoy his presence. Days working with young people pay a very rich reward, as their lives may transform nations and generations to come.

I am older and wiser now. If Hazel had written this chapter, she would tell of the cost to my health and my unintentional neglect of my family and friends.

I am convinced that some marriages stay together for the sake of the ministry. Too frightened to admit their marriage has failed, pastors and their spouses keep up the pretence of intimacy. By throwing themselves into the frenetic activity of caring for others, pastors may divert their attention away from home, choosing to be loved by the congregation rather than nurturing and protecting the love of spouse and family. It is here that the flesh and world meet in a deadly combination. My broken flesh needs the approval of others and is not satisfied with the love of those who truly matter. In its fallen state, human desire cannot rightly distinguish between what it needs and what it wants. As James states in 4:2, "You desire but do not have." So what do you do? You covet. Money, love, sex, status, approval, and recognition are deadly attractions. A worldly shopping list of pleasure that is short-lived.

Think. Do you want to live in the world, or act like the world? The tension we face is that we are called to love our spouses, families, congregations, and communities with the same intense and indiscriminate love. But the models we pursue have often been shaped by the world, and in that world such expressions range from the noble to erotic. We can rarely protect ourselves against their advances when we live without God.

The problem is that the flesh cannot resist the world. But the good news is that the Holy Spirit can. That is why it is critical that we be immersed in the Holy Spirit. And as James implores, we must submit to God and be controlled by his impulses. To be controlled by the Spirit keeps our own impulses in check. The model of love we need is found in the covenant heart of God. Agape love is that great, faithful, and unconditional love of a perfect heavenly Father. When such love becomes our daily blueprint, we love our wives, congregations, and communities with a love that does not require anything other than their permission. Our desire to love is not based on others' response but on the opportunity to give without return. Only the Spirit of God can produce such a desire and retain such a balance in our lives. When the Spirit nurtures this love, no one is neglected, least of all those whom God has gifted to us with that special relationship.

CHAPTER ELEVEN

Standing on the Edge of Change

First Ballymena church had considered extending my associateship for another three years. The prospect of another term brought sheer delight and the opportunity of a more settled life. But in 1999, the minister, Ronnie Hetherington, left to become minister of Glengormley. His departure left Hazel and me with a major question: Does God want us to stay on until a new minister arrives, or is he creating other opportunities for us to consider?

Hazel and I pray and read together usually before she leaves for work each morning. One particular morning our Bible notes took us to the story of Abraham. His call had been into the unknown, yet he had abandoned himself to the process of trusting God. We sensed a note of caution in the reading, with the hint that God was going to move us outside our comfort zone.

We had become comfortable in First Ballymena. Though the work was a challenge, we had grown deeply in love with the congregation. The young people were like our family. They were often at our house on Sunday nights, and our door was always open to them. We would have loved nothing more than to stay at the church, but we couldn't ignore the disquiet and restlessness we felt. I don't think we objected to a little bit of discomfort, but we did not expect its removal altogether.

On the day that God started to move the process forward, I was out visiting. Hazel was at home when the telephone rang. She missed getting the call, so she dialled 1471 to recall the last number.

She had trained with a girl from Newtownards so she recognised the area code. Ringing the person back, she learned it was the Reverend William Sinclair, who was in charge of the vacancy in Strean congregation. He requested that I call him back when I returned. As soon as Hazel hung up, she burst into tears, certain that I was going to be called to Newtownards. Later she confessed a desire not to tell me about the telephone call, but, of course, she felt compelled to give me the message. Nervously I rang the number and a soft and gracious tone responded, "Alistair, Scrabo Presbyterian is vacant."

Now, Scrabo had never featured on my radar. I was a County Antrim man who rarely ventured into County Down, other than my very pleasant stay in Kilkeel. In fact, I hadn't a clue where Scrabo was. I had been in Newtownards once and while there received a parking ticket, so I wasn't best predisposed to its residents, or at least to one particular traffic warden.

"I really don't know anything about Scrabo," I said.

"Why don't you think about it and give me a ring back? Twelve people have shown an interest in it," he said.

"Leave it with me." And so ended our conversation.

At that time, I was interested in Woodlands Presbyterian, which is in Carrickfergus, and Legacurry Presbyterian, outside Lisburn. Hazel and I decided to go down and have a look at these churches—at least drive past them. Upon reaching Carrickfergus, we drove into the car park at Woodlands. The church was open, so we decided to take a look. We met somebody at the door, who showed us around the premises. We thought the church was brilliant. We were especially encouraged by its potential and the opportunity to reach out into the community.

In consideration of William's call, we decided to drive to Scrabo Presbyterian. We thought it might be near Scrabo Tower, an idyllic black stone building from the 1800s. We drove up towards the tower, but we couldn't see a church anywhere. However, we spotted a housing estate down to our left. We thought the church might be in there. We stopped at a garage and asked the man for directions. "Yes, the church is located on a housing estate called the Westwinds," he said.

Armed with this new knowledge, we drove down the Comber Road and turned right into the housing estate. We drove around it, viewed the area, then drove back out. The journey home was marked by silence.

We were paralysed by a sinking feeling. We had found the church. We didn't want to speak about it. We could not form the words to express our fears and feelings. If this were it, then our comfort zone was rapidly vanishing. We had seen every mural and drove past every red, white, and blue flagstone. The gunmen painted on the walls followed us with their dark, icy stares. The church looked if it had been built on a budget. I was wrestling with the fact that I was not only a disciple of Jesus but also a husband and a father. We had just secured a place at nursery school for our daughter, and Hazel was pregnant with our son. My decision not only affected my wife but my family's future environment and security, which would both shape and influence my children. What if they grew up to espouse the values those gunmen represented?

Later, Hazel revealed that as we travelled home, it became clear to her that God was calling us to Scrabo. At that point, I had no idea, no sense of peace, desire, or calling to it. Our readings continued to confirm that God was going to place us in a challenge, but his power would be sufficient for such a task.

As the days progressed, I telephoned William and consented to the interview. Hazel was now nine months pregnant with our son, so they brought the interview forward, so as not to clash with her due date.

Each candidate for interview was kept separate, so as

to conceal their identities from one another. The interview room was sparse but brightly lit. The attempt at creating an informal environment within an austere setting was marginally successful but did little to ease my apprehension. With the pleasantries over, it soon became apparent that the elders and I differed on some key areas. In those days, I was opposed to women holding the office of ministers and elders. Scrabo had seven elders, two of which were women. During the interview, I was strategically placed between both of them. As each elder asked a question, I answered in as open, honest, and transparent manner as possible. I believed that if I was honest, they might not call me; then the rejection would be God's responsibility.

William, who had chaired the meeting, telephoned me within hours of my completing the interview. "The elders have selected a list of three candidates, and guess what, Alistair? You are one of them!"

Part of the process of choosing a minister involves the candidates preaching in a morning service. The morning I was scheduled to preach was one of the worst, most disorganised days of our lives. We had two children by this stage—our son Josh was only weeks old—and Hazel couldn't decide whether or not to come with me. First she decided yes, she would come. Then she changed her mind and wouldn't come. And then she was! Finally, with all the Christian grace at my disposal (she may recall it differently), I said, "Are you coming to Scrabo, or not?" Then our son needed to be changed again.

The service started at 10.30 a.m., and I still had to collect something from First Ballymena before going to

Newtownards. We finally left First Ballymena at 9.45. We had set ourselves quite a challenge considering the sixty-two kilometres we had to travel! Despite the significant number of traffic lights between Belfast and Newtownards, we never hit a red light. Was having a green light the whole way an omen? I was too busy watching the road to reflect too deeply on its divine significance. We reached our destination at 10.27 to find the Clerk of Session, David McDowell, and William Sinclair pacing the tarmac awaiting our arrival.

I jumped out of the car, and they basically hurried me in through the back door. I didn't have time to think. I just went straight out and led the service. I preached my prepared sermon.

At a human level, the morning service had gone fairly well. No one had fallen asleep during the sermon or shook their head in obvious disagreement. Some, whilst glancing in both directions, as if fearful of detection, had quietly indicated their approval of my message. Was this a coded acknowledgement they would be voting for me? Mercifully, I was the last of the three candidates to preach and the next night the voting members of the congregation would select which candidate they preferred, later that evening their decision would be announced to those who had gathered.

We stayed in for lunch and tea at my cousin Mervyn's house as he lived in a town nearby. It had been a lovely afternoon, and I quietly comforted myself that if I got the call, I at least could see him more often.

The following evening Hazel and I attended a dinner party with a few friends. I had given our host's telephone number to William Sinclair should he need to contact me.

The phone rang while were eating dinner. All guests knew I was expecting the call, so all conversation stopped. My heart pounded as I rose from my seat and went to another room to take the call. When I returned, all eyes were on me. It was an awkward moment, and I didn't feel much like eating desert.

The call was issued. After Hazel and I discussed our decision, we accepted and arrived in Scrabo in January 2000. From a worldly perspective, it was a difficult decision to make. We had considered three churches, and from a human perspective they offered what Scrabo could not. The work in First Ballymena had gone well, and they had asked me to extend my contract. I felt I had unfinished business with the young people and had been keen to explore new ministries and opportunities. I would like to have seen my children grow up in a town close to where I was raised.

In human terms, I was the least known of all the three candidates who preached to the congregation. Yet the call of God is not fashioned or controlled by human impulses or reasoning. God had issued the invitation and I had accepted the call. The truth was, I was not equipped to deal with the challenge. God would put me to the test, and for a season I fell woefully short.

CHAPTER TWELVE

Standing in the Link Corridor

We arrived at Scrabo in January 2000, but not all at once. The manse was undergoing renovation, and we had no kitchen and no beds. Our youngest was thirteen weeks old, and the house was full of tears and tantrums—mostly, but not exclusively, his. Because this living situation was not conducive to family life, especially with a new baby, I remained in our new home, and the family would return a week later. To facilitate my situation, Hazel intended to arm me with an airbed and clothing. As I waved at Hazel disappearing into the night, it dawned on me that the only thing in my hand was the backdoor key. I had no bed and no change of clothes. I felt my halo slip ever so slightly.

This was before mobile phones were in common use, so I would have to wait until morning to contact her. I muttered as I turned the key in the door. At least I could get in from the cold. As I swung the door open, a wall of cold hit me. The manse was colder inside than the subzero temperature outside. I was told the oil tank would be full so that I could fire up the central heating system; however, I found a note on the porch from the oil delivery man. The tanker couldn't make it up the drive, and he would not return until Wednesday. No heat had been on in the house for over a year, and this was mid-January.

The weather wasn't the only thing hovering at the freezing point. My attitude was beyond frosty. I had no change of clothes, only the suit I wore. I had no bed. I tried to sleep on the floor in a freezing cold house. My nose had never been so red, and the sweet Christmas carols sung weeks before about the newborn Saviour having no place to lay his head brought little comfort. The best I did was to lament that when God said he would take me out of my comfort zone, I didn't think he meant taking away my mattress too.

I contacted Hazel in the morning and stressed that I needed a change of clothes, and, yes, a bed might be nice.

It was a frostbitten Sunday morning when I preached my first sermon as Scrabo Presbyterian's new minister. I didn't inform the congregation of my current living situation because I had only just arrived and wanted to be on my best behaviour. After all, my miserable, freezing, sleepless night wasn't their fault.

My previous church had a regular attendance of about 500, so seeing only eighty or so congregants on that first Sunday morning left me feeling incredibly low. More people had turned up to hear me preach during the vacancy than had returned to hear me as their new minister. I think the attendance was eighty-seven, including only three or four children. The congregation was lovely, but looking back, I felt in some way that I wasn't ready for this church. Though I didn't realise it at the time, a big, steep learning curve loomed ahead for me.

For two or three months, I went through the motions of preaching. My sermons did not lack substance, but they were missing heart. Some of my colleagues had the luxury of rotating praise bands for their worship services, but Scrabo's only musician was Ian. He had a real heart for Jesus and worship, but that brought me little comfort. We had few, if any, instrumental resources to use or build on, so we supplemented the worship with midi files.

We lived in the middle of a housing estate of 2,500 people, but our church's congregation was a mere eighty-plus. In my darkest thoughts, I genuinely believed God had called the wrong person. I was frightened, frustrated, and powerless to bring about the necessary changes. More than once I thought, "These people are lovely, but I want to go back to Ballymena."

Every Sunday for three months I stepped into Scrabo Presbyterian's pulpit and performed my duty, but my heart and soul were miles away.

Spring had arrived, but my heart remained in winter's chill. The season of humbling was bleak and painful. I had arrived in Scrabo believing myself to be God's gift to the nation. If the congregation truly understood my gifts and talents, they should be grateful that God had called me to such a place. Looking back, my arrogance makes me blush with embarrassment, but truth be told, back then I had refused to listen to God. He wanted to teach me so much, but until I was willing to learn, his lessons fell on deaf ears and a heart that refused to believe I had anything to learn.

On one particular Sunday morning, I stood on the platform and looked out over my little congregation. I had yet to throw myself on God, trusting him to guide me as I led these good people. In fact, I was relying on my strength, gifts, and self-generated resources. Truthfully, I was sinking. As a result, I began to feel sorry for myself. I even lost sight of my family. Everything had all become about me. I no longer even recognised who I was. I felt like a big piece of me was dying, and I blamed it on the church, my environment, even God. But these were not killing me. I was killing myself. I had allowed envy into my thinking. When one becomes engrossed in himself and not in God, he is in danger of losing his blessing. This was where I was. I became jealous of others, whom I thought were less talented than I yet seemed to be in better situations. Inwardly, I bemoaned the fact that people I had trained with were in what I deemed healthier churches and ministries than I was. Along with envy and jealousy came resentment. The battle within had robbed me of joy, and if I were not careful, it would rob me of God's presence altogether. My own self-perceived importance was crushing me. In spiritual terms, I was in heart failure.

During my first three months in Scrabo's pulpit, I delivered flawless sermons. My theology was spot-on. I clearly and logically conveyed the text's meaning. However, I failed to connect with the congregation. I failed because I was losing my connection with God. My gradual decline in spiritual health had reached the critical level. That is, until one morning. I was standing in what they called the "link corridor", a little passageway that joins the Minister's Room to the main church. While waiting to preach, God spoke to me as clearly as if he were standing in the room: *Alistair, how long do you want to do this?*

"Lord, I don't even want to do it until next Sunday. I really don't have anything to contribute."

Alistair, you can either do this with me or without me. It is your choice.

It really was as stark as that. God had turned up in the link corridor, and his message was unmistakable: This either happens with me or without me. I knew in my heart that if I continued trying to lead Scrabo Presbyterian as I had been, in my own strength, God would let me fall. On the other hand, if I were willing to accept his help, then maybe my heart would recover.

I fell to my knees. The words of that chorus were never as true as in that moment, "melt me, mould me, fill me, use me." James 4:8 speaks of purifying your heart. When God decides that holy fire is the only appropriate method of arresting our attention, it is a painful experience. But if we genuinely want to do battle against the flesh and stand defiant against worldly attitudes, it is a necessary one. Moulding me and filling me may be required later, but in that moment I had to become a cleansed vessel.

That's when my ministry at Scrabo really began.

CHAPTER THIRTEEN

Standing Back to Watch God Do Extraordinary Things

Shortly after my encounter with God in the link corridor, the elders called a session meeting to review all our work within the congregation.

Our first discovery was that attendance was declining at a rate of 4.5 percent a year. This concerned us because the Presbyterian denomination was declining at a slower rate of only 3.7 percent, but we were exceeding that figure. We calculated that if this figure remained, in the not too distant future we would have an average attendance of a mere fifty-six people at Sunday morning worship, despite being in the centre of a large housing estate. Declining at such a rate, our hope for growth seemed out of reach.

This realisation was devastating. It produced a stunned silence. We were at a loss as to know what to do. However, our prayer was simple, “Lord, we are throwing ourselves on you.”

We knew we had to make changes, but what they should be was a mystery. Vision cannot be secured in an instant; it takes time to cultivate and often we must take baby steps towards transformation and change.

David McDowell, our Clerk of Session, was not a man to endorse unnecessary change, but when he considered the need for change, he was willing to explore every biblical option. As we considered how we had been conducting the services, we identified a few areas of concern. Our worship was too formal and the style not conducive for those with young families. On some occasions Sunday school teachers returned to their homes because they had no children to teach. It appeared we had given up the expectation of young mothers attending worship, for we had ignored their needs. The only toys to be found on a Sunday were stashed in a ripped cardboard box in the smallest room in the building that was little more than a storage room for cards and stationary—certainly not an inviting and comfortable room for mums and babes. Overall, the facilities had become a little tired and dated.

Yes, we were willing to change. But what were those changes to be?

I stumbled upon a book entitled *Rediscovering the Church: The Story and Vision of Willow Creek Community Church* by Lynne and Bill Hybels. I had never heard of Willow Creek, and I am not entirely sure why it caught my eye. No one had recommended it to me, and I had never read any reviews about it. I simply picked it off the shelf and purchased it. Whenever I read, I often look ahead to see how many pages I have left to read before I reach the end of the chapter and can put it down. But not this book. As I read each page, I could not wait to get to the next chapter. God's timing was perfect—it always is. In the link corridor, he had promised to do something at Scrabo; now he was showing me what could be done.

Through Hybels's book and God's intervention, I received the inspiration of what church could look like if we were passionate about change. If we could understand how to become a church within the community, we might see the power and presence of God at work. We had been a church in the community but had not really explored in any great depth how to be a church for the community. Previous ministries had established a desire, but I think we felt for the first time that we had a genuine opportunity to effect change in the lives of the residents, thus affecting the entire community. Critically, we began to explore ways of engaging with the community, seeking to win their trust before we could win their hearts. The first thing we did was introduce All-Age Family Service to connect with the community. We explored ways of communicating the message that became more interactive and relevant to the listening skills of those we desired to reach.

With this in mind, we borrowed a data projector for that service so we could produce a more visual service for families. We bought puppets from America and put together a drama team. We flooded the community with literature, using the opportunity to visit every house in our parish covcring 5000 people. Ian Hanna explored, developed, and enhanced the heart of worship. I joined a housing forum and community association so that I could listen to the problems of housing, health, education, and antisocial behaviour. I attended the local school more frequently and became much more visible within the community

Within two years, congregational attendance had risen from an average of 87 to 140, increasing to as many as 170 at our All-Age Service. Yet only the presentation of the message altered and not its content. The drive behind changing our methods of communication emerged from the desire to effectively communicate our message. If people really did matter to God, and we believed they did, then they deserved our best efforts in delivering that message in an intelligible way. And whilst there is not always a clear line between relevance and compromise, we did try to avoid jettisoning our integrity in pursuit of numerical growth. Our focus centred on discipleship rather than numerical increase. Although we did believe that if the church was passionate about following Jesus, then possibly others would follow. To our delight they did.

It was important to become a church dispersed in the community, as opposed to a community that came to church.

By making this our emphasis, we avoided making attendance our goal and directed our attention to loving God and our neighbours. It was by growing spiritually that we found, often as a consequence, that we grew numerically as well. Yet even in the midst of this remarkable turnaround, God had much more to teach me.

CHAPTER FOURTEEN

Standing in a Messy Church

During this period of church growth, a mother and her three children started to attend worship. The woman was not in a good place in her life. She seemed to be at odds not only with her neighbours but also with herself. She became embroiled in an altercation with a member of the community whose frustration finally bubbled to the surface with the charge, "You need to get your life sorted out! Why don't you try the church?"

Under the compulsion of such forceful evangelism, she did just that!

My family and I had already met her three children. At the time, our daughter was three years old and attended the same church playgroup as this woman's daughter. As little as this girl was, she had learned how to put our daughter in the equivalent of a choke manoeuvre straight from the MMA. I was not within reaching distance to rescue my daughter, so she had to weather this barrage of punches without her dad, a qualified boxing coach, in her corner. This woman's daughter showed promise, and, in fact, if she had a promoter, she would have had a promising fighting career. She delivered a flawless right cross. As a coach I was impressed: she had perfect timing, and her range was almost textbook. Yet, I'm happy to report that my daughter fared well, albeit she needed to pay more attention to her footwork.

The first time the mother arrived at the church service, her three children didn't even know how to sit. They ran around the whole service. But the congregation began to love the mother and look after her little ones. Eventually, she came to me and asked, "Alistair, I know I am not a Christian, but would you say a little prayer of blessing for my children?"

"I would be delighted."

"You know they don't sit very well."

"I appreciate that," I said.

"I don't even know how they would stand at the front as you attempt to say a prayer for them."

"We will sort it out." I smiled, hoping to reassure her . . .

and me.

I scheduled this special prayer for the next All-Age service. Normally, 170 to 180 people crammed into our little building on the estate. But I had selected that Sunday because I wanted to show the community how embracing and welcoming our congregation had become. That was my thinking, but God had a richer agenda.

As I brought the mother and the three children up to the front, I explained to the congregation what I was about to do. We read from Mark 10, about Jesus blessing the little children, and that seemed a good thing for us to do. Then I asked the congregation to bow their heads and we would pray.

The children had other ideas, one of which was that they didn't want to be prayed for. The oldest boy ran off in the direction of the keyboard and played tug-of-war with its lead. The keyboard player helplessly glared at me, clearly signalling that this was my fault and I had better rescue him. I couldn't because the other child had run behind me and found my bag of crepe bandage I was to use as a visual during my children's talk. She then began running around the church, using the bandage as a streamer. Once she'd reached her bother, who continued his tug-of-war amusement, she wound the bandage around him. I glanced at the mother cradling her infant. Her eyes seemed to scream, "I told you so! Now what?"

Everyone in the church seemed shocked and waited for me to do something to regain control. I signalled to a couple of men to grab the children. We quickly corralled them and brought them back to the front. The mother held her baby while firmly gripping her daughter, keeping her at her side. I hung on to the oldest child, who was about four or five years old, and lifted him up into my arms. With all three children held captive, I quickly said—again— "Let's pray." For the second time, the congregation dutifully bowed their heads.

But the moment I said, "Let's pray," and began, the eldest son felt it would be amusing to ram his finger up my nostril, which was more like an uppercut than a poke! Where did these kids learn to box? I wasn't sure whether my nose was bleeding, but reciting the prayer was becoming a problem. People began to raise their heads, knowing that the second prayer had also been aborted. What made it worse was that as I attempted to relieve the anxiety of the moment, the infant vomited. I'm not sure what my expression was, but glancing at the mother I saw her absolutely distraught and overpowered by embarrassment. As the child retched, she bent forward and let out an expletive nurtured by the sheer humiliation of the moment. She'd said it soft enough that only I should have heard it; however, when she leaned over, her mouth came close to my lapel microphone. I'm sure many of the attendees heard her expression, but I was too frightened to catch the eye of any parishioner. Not only had I given no prayer of blessing, the liturgy now included swearing in the Order of Service!

At that point, I just prayed and dealt with the situation as best I could. One elder had further concerns in the aftermath. Her distress stemmed not from the fact that an expletive had been used or that I had failed to pray for someone; rather, her anguish was because the child had vomited over the crepe bandage, the same bandage I had used to mummify her during the children's talk. She had a distinct smell of sick as she was being wrapped from head to toe in this ruined cloth.

After the service, I shook hands with people as they went out the door, but I kept my head bowed. I didn't really look at anybody, nor did I want to engage in conversation.

But God was about to show me something in all of this.

For the next three days, I drove through the housing estate feeling sorry for myself. "Can I not conduct a prayer? Can I not conduct a service?" I had all these people gathered into church and it was just a shamble. The message to the community was that we were out of control. It meant that we couldn't cope. We wanted people from the world to be in church, but we couldn't cope with the fact that they still acted like the world when they joined us for worship. It meant that we didn't know what we were doing or how to cope with it. But I rationalised it all in the plural, when in fact the most honest admission would have been in the singular. It meant that I didn't know what I was doing and that I didn't know how to cope.

As I was driving up and over one of the speed ramps, God once again prompted my heart. *If you don't want people like that, I won't send them.*

Whoa. I stopped the car. I felt shameful for the attitudes I had harboured. The truth hit me: that service had actually been more about what I was doing and less about what God was attempting to do.

We prayed for that woman and her family, we loved her, and we kept that girl in church until eventually she was forced to leave the estate seven months later because of further altercations.

But through our time of caring for a family in crisis, we learned that we needed to have a heart for God and that our job was to love people for who they were, not what we wanted them to be. So what if she had sworn into my lapel microphone? God was big enough to accept the brokenness of that situation and to use even that event for his own glory. It had been an opportunity for us to display a genuine and authentic care for a mother and her three children. Her life had been a very difficult mess. She was broken and needed love and a huge lot of understanding.

People talk about "messy church" today. With the greatest respect, the term is often used in middle-class churches seeking to make a connection with the brokenness around them. Yet it is these very same middle-class churches where individuals frequently keep up appearances and pretend that their lives are together. We do not create a messy church by scheduling into an hour on Sundays. Truth is, we are a messy church. The church at Corinth was an example of a messy church. The church is at its best when messy people find a loving God and let him fix them. The best churches are those who invite messy people into their lives and not to an event. How can those who are hurting see God fixing your brokenness if they cannot meet the real you? What is so often presented at an event or on a Sunday is a far cry from how Christians live on Monday through Saturday. But when people live in a community on a housing estate, it is impossible to hide or conceal who they really are.

Let non-Christians see God restoring you. We are not mess-free, but by God's grace we are becoming less messy and more Christ-like. Be vulnerable: let a non-Christian see that you are a work in progress, and introduce them to the gospel-loving, grace-giving God that he is.

So began a journey for our church, one that is still progressing to this day. God had said to me: "You can either do this with me or without me." God was turning up and doing his work regardless of what we still had to learn. In his mercy, he was using our weaknesses to reach out to people. One of the most profound lessons the church learned was to weep with those who weep.

CHAPTER FIFTEEN

Standing in Awe

The church is not a building or something Christians "do." Church is the fellowship of believers living and growing in faith and relationship with Christ. As such, God showed us that he could move outside the building with or without our assistance.

Enter Tommy and Roberta. Tommy had worked at Harland and Wolfe, famous for building the *Titanic.* He had worked a hard job on the bough of ships, in confined spaces, and in poor conditions. Now retired, he was in his late sixties. A former boxer, he had no interest in church whatsoever. He hadn't been to a service in thirty or forty years, except for the obligatory weddings and funerals.

Out of the blue one Sunday morning, whilst lying in bed, he said to his wife, "Roberta, I have got to go to church today."

"What?!"

"The church down on the estate. I don't know, I just need to go, Roberta."

She threw back the covers and got out of bed. "Well, if you are going, so will I."

That morning and the next two weeks, Tommy and Roberta came to church and sat on the back row. After the service on the third week, as I shook his hand before he left the service, he said, "Alistair, one Sunday when you were preaching, I just wanted to get up and dance. The joy of God came over me in a way I had never experienced before. I knew nothing about it except that this huge load was lifting off my shoulders. Other than the fact that my legs were going and Roberta had to keep me in my seat, I would have got up and danced."

Both he and Roberta gave their lives to the Lord. That someone wanted to dance in a Presbyterian church had nearly overshadowed the content of the entire conversation. He thought of joy, whereas, I feared the possibility of a Kirk Session meeting required too justify his actions.

During this same period, God spoke to another lady on the estate. *You have got to go to church*. She obeyed and made her way to our building. She, too, heard the gospel, saw her need, and got saved.

God's actions demonstrated a very clear message: He can save people anywhere, with or without our help. He has the power to call men and women out of houses, factories, and war-torn communities to embrace his love and grace. How wonderful it is to have the privilege of being used in God's redemptive plans! Yet we must assume this role with humility and never with arrogance.

God had given Scrabo Presbyterian Church a gentle nudge to get out into the community and show his love. We visited every home with the *Jesus* video, spoke with many residents, and often implored them to come to church. God may have been pleased with our efforts, but he was not compelled to use them. Some days he just wants us to stand back and recognise that he is God and we are not. God alone has the power to save. I am more convinced today than ever before that God is always more pleased with my obedience rather than my efforts.

A number of years ago I was asked to write an article for a magazine. Its remit was fairly clear: an outline to readers as to the reasons for church growth, particularly how it related to our experiences at Scrabo. I thought I wrote a fairly good article, until I read it again. The article inadvertently overstated our human role in the transformation. There is a real temptation to believe that the formulation of vision plans, strategic practices, and human giftedness play a greater part than they do in the fruitfulness of a church. It is not to say that God can't use these; because of his grace he often will.

But the world uses these very same policies and acquisitions, too. I am convinced that most CEOs could grow a church numerically, but they may fail to develop it spiritually. We are most at danger when a combination of the flesh and world shape our thinking. We cannot always avoid some of the world's fingerprints smudged over our motivations, but we can avoid its ever-tightening grip. If the world's clutches can be detected in our motives and practices, then our successes may be short-lived. We could have a megachurch but then soon find that it has been built on extremely shallow foundations. A church shaped by worldly practices may effect changes, but those changes are fleeting. Only a church governed, empowered, and led by the Spirit will bring about permanent transformation. That is why Jesus implored Nicodemus in John 3 to be born from above, not from below. All our thinking and actions must go through those regenerative processes, too.

PART THREE: THE DEVIL

Be alert and of sober mind, your enemy the devil prowls around like a roaring lion looking for someone to devour.

1 Peter 5:8

When your life is in a state of disrepair and the world is forlorn and grey, the last thing you need is an enemy. One such Enemy stands head and shoulders above all others. His name is Satan, and in an effort to destroy us, he will exploit our personal vulnerabilities and collective weaknesses. He is manifested in corrupted political systems and in societies caught up in hate, prejudice, and war. He will use collective and personal greed so that children are sold as slaves and used in the porn industry. He will provide rationalisations for the misuse of power that keeps women suppressed and the poor marginalised. We can see his dirty fingerprints all around our world as he sets up idols of materialism, individualism, atheism, and every other manifestation of sin where humans seek to live independently from God. But what when his presence, or that of his demonic forces come closer to home? When he is not hiding in the structures of our broken world or when he tempts us to err and sin? What happens when, as in the story of the three little pigs, the big bad wolf comes? When he stands at your door and confidently says, "I'm going to huff, and puff and blow your house down." What resilience will we show then? In order to see our Enemy take to his heels, he must be resisted. We may even lose a few rounds as we trade punches, but with God's grace we will emerge victorious at the final bell.

> Submit yourselves, then, to God. Resist the devil, and he will flee from you.
>
> James 4:7

CHAPTER SIXTEEN

Standing with the Shield of Faith

By mid-year 2000, Scrabo Presbyterian's congregants were basking in a time of unprecedented blessing. No experience on earth compares with the joy and peace of hearing God's Word and singing his praise.

During my first two years as the church's pastor, we underwent numerical growth, but far more important, enriching, and lasting was the spiritual growth of individuals and a united church. We were experiencing God in a fresh and meaningful way. We moved from using midi files and supplementing music to a live praise group. Our attendance increased in all services: worship, midweek Bible study, and children's ministry. We had enough youth attending that warranted starting a youth fellowship. We rejoiced with those who had received salvation, and we gained a genuine desire to embrace the community around us. We welcomed everyone into our fellowship.

But we should have been cautious not to embrace everyone.

We failed to recognise the Enemy of our souls, who arrives in many shapes and forms. I may have been learning to subdue the flesh, to cleanse my motivations, and to purify my heart. I may even have waged war against the principles that govern this broken world. But dark clouds were forming on the horizon. I could hear distant footsteps of an altogether different enemy.

The Prince of Darkness had arrived.

When God is at work, the Enemy, Satan, always seeks to move in and steal our peace, joy . . . anything good God has brought into which is at the heart of this book.

Expelled from heaven for his arrogant desire to be God, Satan carries a grudge of unmatched proportions. The greater the elevation, the harder the fall, and he has nursed the wounds of his humiliation ever since. His giftedness now coupled with his resentment makes him the deadly opposition that he is. In Ezekiel 28:18 we read, "Your heart became proud on account of your beauty, and you corrupted your wisdom because of your splendour. So I threw you to the earth; I made a spectacle of you before kings."

Beauty and wisdom are great attributes, and although Satan was expelled from heaven, we have no reason to doubt that he retains both. Except for one poisonous alteration: his wisdom is now corrupted. That is why Paul warns 2 Corinthians 2:11 that we should not be unaware of his schemes. And according to Scripture, he is a scheming liar. This thief has the resolute intent of robbery, death, and destruction. He will use his beauty and remaining wisdom to bring about your demise. He trades on his beauty to avoid detection. How can someone so beautiful be so violent? Because he feels humiliated by the Lord of all creation. He interprets his being made a spectacle as a betrayal. Knowing that he forfeited the Fathers' love, he is jealous of the love the Father showers on us. Having lost everything, he leaves destruction in his wake. His one last defiant stand is believing that to hurt us is to hurt God. He is going to hell and he is intent on taking the world with him.

His dominion was under threat as we had taken the gospel to our community. Our attendance was growing primarily through conversions with an average attendance of 140 people. Christians were flourishing and their knowledge of the Bible was growing. The people were learning to support and love one another and giving financially, which demonstrated their gratitude to God. God's presence in our services and in the congregants' lives was real. Perhaps Satan had noted our dependency on God.

I can identify three distinct periods when the Enemy attacked us . . . and with devastating consequences. The first started in November 2000 and continued to June 2001. It began by receiving unsolicited phone calls at the manse. The telephone would ring, and either Hazel or I would lift the receiver and be greeted with silence. They varied in frequency but would happen at least two or three times a week during the day, and even at night. Then paranormal activity in the manse began, marked by doors banging, widows opening, and footsteps being heard running along the first-floor landing.

The concerns I had regarding the manse were now intensified by growing concerns I had at church.

Some of the new Christians were beginning to struggle with doubts, wondering if God had forgiven them and fearing that they would never be able to maintain their Christian experience. I had expected this, as those experiences are common to new believers, but the intensity of doubt and fear alarmed me. It seemed to come in waves, affecting not just a few, but many of those who had committed themselves to Christ. Friction was popping up in the most unlikely of places. Worship, getting into God's presence, became a struggle and a source of concern. Even among the members of the praise groups, tensions emerged. Some members of the church felt isolated or marginalised. Those not elected to lead the congregation felt they should have a greater say in how the church was run.

During this time, I visited an elder at his home. He broke down in inconsolable sobbing, not knowing why he was so depressed.

Clearly, the church had hit a wall, and I didn't know why or how we were going to navigate around it.

One day I picked up Hazel outside the toy and book library of the local school. When I pulled up, she was talking with someone. As soon as she got into the car, she said, "Whatever you do, do not let that person over the door of our house."

The force of her words startled me. "Why? What are you talking about?"

"I don't know. I just feel a real oppression, and something is not right."

I took her warning to heart. I knew something was wrong, but I didn't know what.

Sometime later I was reading the Bible while sitting in the front room of the manse. A verse of Scripture grabbed my attention. It was like a neon sign. The verse weighed on me. Although I wasn't aware of it at the time, I actually misread the verse. I read the phrase from Psalm 91:3 as "I will deliver you from the net." It actually reads "I will deliver you from the trap."

I drove around the estate for three days, unable to shake the verse from my heart. How could this very real heaviness I was feeling come from such a wonderful promise?

A few days later, Hazel sat down with me at the kitchen table. "Alistair, I am going to say something to you and I want you to hear me through." Knowing I regarded visions and dreams as unnecessary additions to the power of God's Word, she approached me cautiously.

Immediately, my scepticism indicator kicked into

high gear. "Go ahead, explain what you think God has said to you though this dream."

"In the dream, I was standing, watching Scrabo Presbyterian. All of a sudden, a net descended over the church. I thought it was a net of protection, but then in the dream I was asked to swivel round. As I did, that girl I was talking to when you picked me up was standing with her arms folded and a smug expression on her face." Hazel was adamant. "I thought it was a net of protection but it's not, and that's all that I can say to you."

Hazel hadn't known that God had already spoken to me through his Word, and that verse had been tormenting me for days. God had spoken to me independently through his Word and to Hazel through a dream. I became convinced that the church was now in a period of bondage, and the Enemy was seeking to stifle what God had sought to do. I didn't know what to do about it, why it was a problem, and why, in particular, this girl was a problem.

Not long after Hazel's dream, I learned that before this girl had joined our church, she had been in a coven. One evening an email arrived in my inbox. Somehow I had been copied into it along with the primary recipient, a warlock in Belfast. This girl was asking that she be permitted to relinquish her contact with them. Not too many minutes after receiving the first email, I received a second. She maintained that I had been copied in by mistake. I doubted this was true, as my name and the warlock's were a sufficient distance from each other in the alphabet. I now believe that she wished to disguise her intentions.

I did not feel comfortable sharing this with the eldership, as we were in the early days of our ministry together. I was truly frightened that they wouldn't believe me. That to make such revelations would undermine my credibility. I felt that some elders were on their own spiritual journey, and that our growing relationships of trust could be so easily jeopardised. I was trying to ascertain what they believed about God, let alone determine what they believed about Satan. I had also reacted against the charismatic movement, and this type of experience only reminded me of what I had previously rejected. I had made such a big deal of my Reformed position whilst a student at Elim Bible College, and to admit that God had spoken to us in this way was tantamount to a public retraction of my Reformed position. In short, I was also concerned that it just sounded weird.

My greatest regret is that I didn't do what Hazel asked. This person did arrive at our manse, I allowed her in, and, as a result, the environment changed.

Her arrival brought physical manifestations of the Enemy's war against God's righteous saints. Satan took the war against Scrabo Presbyterian to an altogether different and frightening level. Do I believe she was the cause of all that happened? Probably not. She may not have been conscious of the impact of her presence. However, a doorway to danger had been opened and I wasn't sure how it would be closed.

I, in particular, was significantly out of my depth. I had little knowledge concerning spiritual warfare and even less experience. I knew we were in trouble. But I also knew that God had not left us defenceless. The truth of Ephesians became our daily experience: "We wrestle not against flesh and blood but against principalities and powers and spiritual wickedness in high places" (Ephesians. 6:12, author's paraphrase). God had a work for us to do, and it became necessary for us to put on the full armour of God if we hoped to withstand Satan's attacks and to be left standing at all.

If ever God was going to take the members of Scrabo Presbyterian out of our comfort zone, this was now the fulfilment of our Father's promise. Yet no matter how much bewilderment or confusion we experienced, we fully believed that God remained in charge. We had his Word on it when he declared, "I will deliver you from the net." I clung to that promise with all my heart, soul, and mind.

CHAPTER SEVENTEEN

Standing Firm in the First Attack

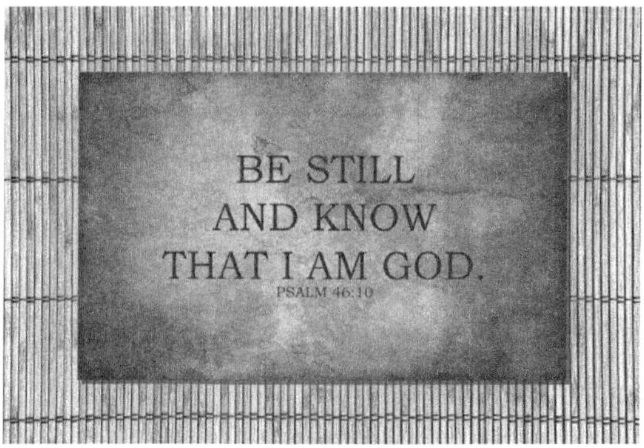

The battle raged for months. We experienced physical manifestations in the manse and spiritual challenges at church. I had been instructed by God through Scripture to "be still and know that [he is] God." My pastor's heart ached as I watched people suffering and yet not able to intervene. I was also frightened that my inactivity could be interpreted as lack of concern for people. I knew that this girl's presence may have been responsible for some of their problems, but I could not say why I believed her presence to be a problem. In terms of the flesh and human logic, early intervention would have relieved the suffering of others. But God, once again, required submission so that I would cultivate the qualities of trust and patience, believing that God's intervention is based on his perfect timing.

Also, if I had sought to explain to the leadership about my distress, they may have interpreted my position as a personal dislike of this individual, which actually would not have been true. I thought that the risk of divulging this information could have been divisive and had the potential to split the church. If we had selected her for censure, some may have regarded our actions as harsh and inappropriate. By God asking me to wait, he was developing my capacity to be as gentle as a dove and wise as a serpent. Had I not followed God's instruction completely, I might have applied human wisdom to the situation, as opposed to the wisdom of our heavenly Father. To rush headlong through impatience and provide my own wise counsel at a time that seemed appropriate to me, may have made the circumstances worse. Never before had I needed the levels of wisdom required, but as James 1:5 encourages, "If any of you lacks wisdom, you should ask God, who gives generously to all without finding fault, and it will be given to you." And I needed God to be generous.

As I was praying about this girl's involvement in church, I believe God required my patience because he, not I, would expose their sin in public. I could not suppress this deep impression given by God, though it seemed a little confusing. I knew that this girl had admitted her previous involvement in a coven, but I was also aware that she had acted alone. However, God had given me the word *their involvement,* and I was not sure what this meant.

One summer day in August we had just pulled our car into the driveway after a well-earned holiday. I had to forcibly push open the front door of the manse, as a mountain of post had wedged it closed. One letter, from Clerk of Session David McDowell, slid off the pile and lay on the floor a little separate from the rest. In it he explained that during my holiday, it had become known that this particular girl and another member of the congregation had been having an affair. God had remained true to his word, "their sin had been exposed in public."

Two elders and I visited her home and gently but firmly explained that her activities were sinful and she was to withdraw from taking Communion until a period of repentance and restoration had occurred. She appeared to be unhappy with our proposals and subsequently left the church.

Was she responsible for all the paranormal activity in our home and at the church? Probably not, as I believe the move of the Holy Spirit had attracted the attention of people more heavily involved in the occult. But I think it serves as a stark reminder that we Christians are locked in a spiritual battle, and like any war, we will undergo dark nights and long days as well as suffer the inevitable casualties.

Often as the intensity of spiritual battle subsides, it is easy to underestimate its impact. I started to think that all the strange occurrences in our home had been a dream, or that the stresses of ministry had predisposed me to read too much into the actions of people at church.

Several years later and a few years after leaving Newtownards, I had an occasion to visit. I decided to drive past the old manse, as I had been told it lay derelict since the church had sold it. I parked the car on the footpath and walked up the driveway. On either side of the big old wooden door were glass panels that ran full length. These had been smashed in. In fact, almost all the windows had been smashed. Broken bottles lay strewn throughout the overgrown grass. I could easily enter the property, so I decided to go in. I stepped onto the porch and froze. I went completely cold. Immediately I sensed a deep impression in my heart to proceed no farther. In a gentle but stern whisper, I felt the Lord say, *Turn and go out.* So I turned, got into my car, and drove out. I put the experience behind me, though I had explained to Hazel the manse's current state of disrepair and my disquiet.

Three weeks later, on a lovely summer evening with the sun splitting the trees, my family and I were travelling to a barbecue hosted by close friends David and Betty. Hazel said, "Why don't we pull over and let the children see what has become of the old property?"

As we stopped in front of the property, we saw a man dressed in a full black robe with hood used by those engaged in the occult. He was standing on the building's first floor flat roof, looking through the window were Hazel and I used to sleep. He appeared to be addressing someone in the room.

The fact that God had prompted me a few weeks earlier not to enter the property now made sense. It is common practice for the occult to desecrate what is often regarded as a holy place. Once again this confirmed to us the intensity of what we had experienced. It was a reminder that this spiritual war continues to rage. The Enemy is never happy when we fearlessly proclaim our allegiance to Christ.

But fearless loyalty demands God's protective armour. How well do you know each piece of armour? Each piece protects something vital in our relationship with God. He defends us against the Enemy, but he also provides us with an offensive weapon: the Bible, God's Word. Few people rely on this weapon today. Consequentially, they are weak in every battle. And in the most intense of conflicts, they are even more vulnerable whilst under attack.

Our church emerged from the battle scarred but victorious. Never again would we begin warfare without God's armour, for the battle is too fierce and intense to go onto the battlefield without it.

I am convinced that as time progressed, had we not received the prayerful support of leaders, friends, and prayer warriors, like; Alan, Sandra, Miriam, Margaret and others, that our spiritual survival would have been under threat. Some of these saints lived in England. Thank God that in spiritual warfare we are not separated by land or sea, but bound together by God's Holy Spirit.

CHAPTER EIGHTEEN

Stand Against the Enemy

The enemy was to return to our home in 2007. This second attack did not involve physical manifestations and the Enemy's party tricks as he done before; rather, it was directed more specifically at me.

One day as I was watching television, I started hearing a ringing noise in my ear. It is common to hear a high-pitched sound in your ears and then for it to disappear.

But this ringing never ended. I eventually went to a doctor, who diagnosed chronic tinnitus with a high-pitched squealing or whistling in both ears. Whilst he was trying to be helpful, he inadvertently said that he had treated someone with the condition who had almost gone mad from this illness. (I am grateful he wasn't on my pastoral team.)

I had always enjoyed nearly perfect health, but this issue affected my quality of life. I am not quick to attribute sickness to the direct activity of Satan. On some occasions it might, but more often it is the result of living in a fallen and broken world. The most disarming thing about illness is that we have little or no control over it. It reminds us of our innate powerlessness to control life. It leaves us feeling vulnerable and weak.

I preach passionately, and it takes quite a lot out of me every Sunday. So I often used Sunday afternoons as a period of recovery. I would sleep for a few hours in the afternoon to regain my energy and strength for the evening service. I had previously easily drifted to sleep and enjoyed a restful sleep. But tinnitus robbed me of that. In fact, my ability to sleep at night also significantly declined. I tried to listen to music so that it would counteract the constant ringing in my ears, but I found myself awake most nights in the quietness of the room listening to a high-pitched scream in my ears.

The strain on my health was being matched by the strain on my ministry. Only Hazel and God knew the level of pressure I was under. I was struggling and needed reassurance from God that everything would be okay.

As I was standing with my customary smile at the

church door shaking hands with those who exited after the morning service, one hand gripped mine. As David Davidson shook my hand, he said, "Alistair, I have got to give you this particular verse." He took a little card from his coat pocket and placed it in my hands. It was from Isaiah 41:10: "Do not be afraid for I am with you. Do not be dismayed for I am your God. I will strengthen you, I will help you. I will hold you up with my victorious right hand." In those words, I realised that God was trying to reassure me. A timely reminder that regardless of what I was contending with, he alone would be my strength.

Perhaps God thinks I am a slow learner because at 10.30 p.m. the same evening, I got a phone call from a young man called Andrew McShane. Andrew had never telephoned me at home before, and his voice sounded rather sheepish. "Alistair, I have put off telephoning you for most of the evening, and I don't want you to think that I am mad, but I believe God has given me a verse for you."

"Two verses in one day. This is interesting," I thought. This had never happened to me before, and now it had happened twice in one day. God must have something important to share with me. "What is it?" I asked.

"The verse is from Isaiah chapter forty-one verse thirteen, 'For I am the lord your God who takes hold of your right hand and says "Do not fear I will help you."'"

Those two verses had come to me as undeniable encouragement.

The following Sunday evening as I was leaving church, Lillian Harris paused at the door before exiting. "Alistair, I believe God has a word for you, and it is from the Psalms." The psalm called me to trust him and be confident in the provision that he alone would make.

The following week Hazel and I were treated to a short break from the daily demands of ministry. We were kindly offered accommodation just outside Dublin for a few days. However, the idyllic setting that would normally have provided peace and quiet did not soothe the restlessness of my heart or lessen the weight of my oppression.

Though these verses brought some comfort, the battle I was in was far from over. While in Dublin, I took an unexpected panic attack, something I never had experienced before. It was one of the most frightening experiences I have ever encountered. Much worse than the physical manifestations of evil in the house, I felt as if I were losing control of the situation. Once again God stepped in with impeccable timing. During that day, I received a text message from David Robinson, Joint Pastor of an Assemblies of God Church in Comber. Amazingly, he sent me the verse from Isaiah 41:10! These people who had shared these verses, all within a matter of weeks, were unaware of the struggle I was engaged in but in obedience to God had given me these verses.

The following evening, November 30, Hazel and I sat down together to read our Bible. We normally read from *Word for Today* in which Bob Gass remarked:

> The temptations that come into your life are no different from what others experience, and God is faithful. He will not allow the temptation to be more

> that you can stand. When you are tempted, He will show you a way out so that you can endure. 'I gave you all power over the enemy and nothing shall by any means hurt you' (Luke 10:19). 'The God of peace will soon crush Satan under your feet, the grace strength and enablement of our Lord Jesus be with you' (Romans 16:20). 'Use every piece of God's armour so that you will be able to resist the enemy in the time of evil so that after the battle you will stand and still be standing firm.' [This is Isaiah 41:10 all over again.] 'Do not be afraid for I am with you. Do not be dismayed; for I am your God. I will strengthen you. I will praise you. I will uphold you with my victorious right hand.

During this short but intense period of attack, God brought the same message to me on five separate occasions and by entirely different means. A card delivered at the church door, a telephone message, a spoken word, a text message, and a devotional reading all had been designed to grab my attention and reassure my troubled spirit. God used several means to minister to this troubled and fragile servant.

I emerged from that personal attack a very different person. I was on the ropes, but God had been in my corner. Like Paul acknowledges in 2 Corinthians 4:7–9, "We have this treasure in jars of clay to show that this all-surpassing power is from God and not from us. We are hard pressed on every side, but not crushed; perplexed, but not in despair; persecuted, but not abandoned; struck down, but not destroyed." What comfort we find in these verses! Perhaps this is what you need to be reminded of today. The dark night of your soul will not last forever.

Whilst contracting tinnitus is the product of living in a broken world, Satan used it to efficiently unsettle me. I no longer have a quiet time, at least not in the literal sense. I read, ponder, reflect, and pray, but it is never in quiet. The noise is loud and constant. For a few years I simply could not rest on Sunday afternoons to recover between sermons. So I went for prayer to seek healing, but the condition remains to this day.

Initially I was irritable and impatient. However, what Satan did not realise is that as God helped me to adjust to the noise, he enabled me to deal with irritation. As a consequence, I deal with general irritations much better today. I am much more patient with people. As I have learned to blot out the sounds in my head, so I have learned to streamline my thoughts, to focus on remaining calm and in control. I have found this to be helpful in difficult situations or times of conflict or confrontation. I have found that it is not so much the circumstances that dictate my responses but how my responses affect the circumstances around me. When I cultivate a much more positive attitude towards my circumstances, they seem to trouble me less. And when that happens, Satan cannot leverage the situation to his advantage. In effect, I am able to disarm him by my response.

But patience, self-control, and positive attitudes are not the only actions that lessen Satan's power.

CHAPTER NINETEEN

Standing in the Armour of Effective Prayer

The third attack struck in 2010. It was massive. Satan changed tactics and did not assault the house or me individually. Instead, he came against my family.

We encountered a time of deep distress, heartache, and dismay. The palpable sense of the Enemy's presence in our home was unmistakable. But we also saw God working for our benefit, to protect each member of our family.

One night while sleeping, I woke up very suddenly. I was immediately fully awake and aware. I felt God say to me: *You need to pray for Hazel.*

I looked over to her. She was fast asleep, with no visible indication that she was in distress. However, I felt such a strong impression that I reached over, placed my hand on top of her head, and prayed: "Whatever you need to do God, please do." I then fell back to sleep.

When Hazel awoke the next morning, I asked, "Were you okay last night?"

"Why do you ask?"

"Well, God woke me up and urged me to pray for you."

She looked me in the eye. "Alistair, last night was terrible. I had a dream, but it felt like much more. The Enemy came and stood over me. Suddenly, a total blackness descended upon me. I knew that I needed God to deliver me from whatever was happening, and I tried to pray and to use Jesus's name, but I couldn't. Then, all of a sudden, I was able to declare Jesus's name. Immediately, I was released and the Enemy retreated. I was at peace again."

It was obvious that my prayer had coincided with the time of her release.

At that point, my theological mind asked a million questions. Why did God not give her the power to issue Jesus's name? Why did he need to wake me and request that I place my hand on Hazel's head and pray? Why should her deliverance have depended upon my response?

Whilst I am still wrestling with these questions, the most satisfactory consideration is that believers comprise the body of Christ. In our vertical relationship, we exalt God; in our horizontal relationships, we edify, encourage, and assist one another in our walk with God. What he requires from his creation is that they obey his promptings. The same question could be raised as to why God sent an angel rather than his Holy Spirit to minister to Jesus in the garden of Gethsemane. Yet in Christ's humility he accepted help and the intervention from one he had created. God uses the interconnectedness of his people and his created order to bring glory and honour to himself.

The usefulness of any soldier is his or her ability to obey commands. God was testing my obedience just as he was reminding Hazel of her dependence upon the body of Christ. I am sure if I had been disobedient, God would have delivered her anyway. However, if God had to use another means, I would have failed in my dependency on him. This was somewhat of a small test to prepare us for what was coming. If he was to take us through the looming difficult battle, nothing short of full dependence on him was required.

The shield of faith was truly required. That night in particular, we learned to lock shields together. He had not only taught us to be confident in him but also drove home that our most effective protection is standing united. When Roman soldiers locked shields in turtle formation, the enemy could drive a chariot over them without causing injury. Yet churches are divided by words, complaints, and criticism. For many, the Enemy has no need of a chariot; a feather will do to bring down the church. However, when we stand together and resist the devil, he will flee. Not forever, but long enough to regroup and recover.

If you want a strong marriage, church, or community, don't use your shield to batter others. Rather, lock them together and stand firm against the Enemy of our souls.

Engaged in a battle with the Enemy, we were praying that God would secure us, help us, and bring our family through this. However, we were beaten down, worn out, and felt like we were losing the battle. We could not find support from any outside agencies, and both Hazel and I were finding it difficult to deal with a particular situation. One evening, Hazel and I dropped onto the sofa in my study, exhausted. The emotional strain we were under was intense. With heavy and broken hearts we wept. I felt that my mental and physical health were at serious risk. Weak, mentally bankrupt, and dangerously disheartened, we cried to the Lord, literally sobbed and pleaded with Him, "Lord, as much as I want to engage in ministry, this has taken us to the point of no return. If you do not sort this situation out, then we are finished." Truly, we had come to the end of our strength. It would be easier for us to abandon what we have been called to do than to carry on.

For the next few days nothing changed. No one came to our aid, no phone calls or text messages with encouraging Scripture verses. I can only describe those days as heavy with darkness. Then before a week had passed since we'd pleaded with God, we saw the situation miraculously and supernaturally turn around. Though we couldn't see it at the time, God was working behind the scenes.

Nevertheless, I was so drained and weary that I was

looking for the easy way out of Scrabo. I had laboured hard and felt it was time to leave.

It wasn't long before such an opportunity arrived. A convenor responsible for a vacant congregation approached me, asking if I was interested in applying. Hazel and I prayed about it. Shortly after his initial contact, he rang again to ask if I had come to any decision. My response was, "We don't feel God has particularly spoken to us yet."

Later, as Hazel and I discussed this telephone call, we found ourselves in disagreement. The tension between us was palpable. We felt that God had remained silent on this opportunity, leaving us unsure as to what to do. We wondered if it would be wrong to go without hearing a clear directive from God. Our lives would be more comfortable elsewhere. This particular church was nearby. Our children would suffer no disadvantage by changing schools. We were frustrated as we wrestled with this. We struggled with feeling that God had remained silent on every approach to him. We were frightened that left to our own choices we could possibly make the wrong decision. If we made our decision according to what looked good or out of desperation, it could have a devastating effect on our ministries. The pressure to make a decision while God was silent was intense.

A few weeks passed since the convenor's initial phone call. Very little time remained to make our decision, which only served to heighten our exasperation. Hazel and I disagreed slightly as to what that decision should be. As a result, our discussion ended with increased tension and my obvious displeasure. Hazel asked me to pray with her, and I refused. "I don't feel much like praying," I grumbled.

As Hazel was about to leave the house, she changed her mind, knowing how important it was that we did not allow the Enemy to get a foothold in our relationship. She was right, so I relented and we prayed together.

Immediately after we prayed, I left and went down to the community office. As I was sitting at my desk, I mulled over what had happened between Hazel and me. I felt a bit guilty about my earlier attitudes. David Davidson arrived at the door. Around seventy years of age, he timidly put his head around the open door and said, "Alistair, I have been reluctant to come and say this to you because I am not sure how you are going to receive it. In fact, I have struggled with it for days, but I must be obedient to God." He paused, seeming to muster courage. Then he continued. "It's a phrase which God has placed in my heart, and it's burning a hole in it. Once I say these words I am going to leave. The words are 'You are not to go.'" And with that he disappeared.

Hazel and I had read Scripture, we had committed this decision about taking another church to the Lord, but we needed something that could not be mistaken for our own manipulation of the Bible, or a human construction to ease our exit from the congregation. Once again, God had used David Davidson, who did not know the context or significance of what he spoke into our lives. David did not know that we had been approached with this invitation; only the convener, that congregation's eldership, and ourselves were aware, yet God spoke to us. He gave us the decision, so we declined.

A year passed since God had clearly told us not to go.

Yet my human spirit still remained restless. I had never before sought out a congregation with the possibility of becoming their minister. But the weariness from the continuous spiritual battle had me thinking, "Maybe now is the time for us to leave."

Lo and behold, opportunities came along to be interviewed for two different congregations. It was immediately clear to me that one of the congregations was not the place for me, and I was extremely relieved that it progressed no further than the initial interview. I wasn't so sure about the other one. But God stepped in and closed the door. I have to admit I was disappointed, yet I recognised the wisdom of his decision and acknowledged it. "Right, God, I must settle my mind and heart. I will go nowhere until you reveal otherwise."

The recent attack of the Enemy had significantly subsided. With the pressure on Hazel and me greatly relieved, we were able to function more normally. And one does not emerge from spiritual warfare unchanged. Though we felt roughed up, we were able to look back and see how God had been with us through it all. Though tired, our spirits were strengthened.

Turning our attention to the future, we felt we were being prepared for many more years in Scrabo. Now heartened by God's intervention, we mentally and spiritually prepared to lead Scrabo into the next phase of ministry.

CHAPTER TWENTY

Learning from Others Who Take a Stand

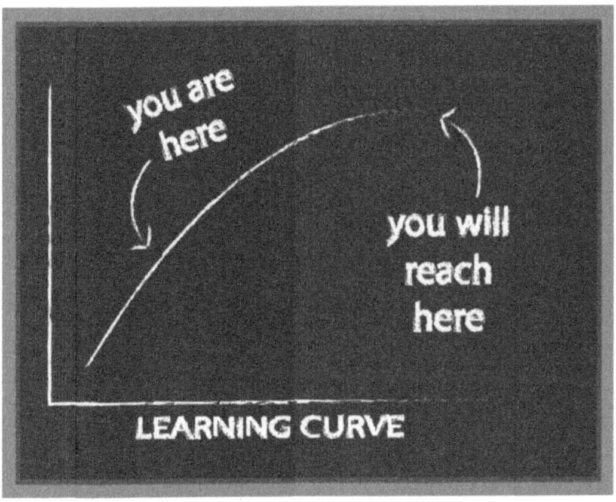

The manse had always been problematic. It was a poorly constructed building, damp, and difficult to heat. The elders and congregants discussed and debated for a number of years as to what to do about it. Some were convinced that it should be sold, whilst others remained unsure. Eventually, the church decided to sell it and use the proceeds to build a new manse. I suppose this could be considered a real blessing! The church was not aware of the Enemy's attack on me personally or his strike against my family while we lived in the manse. To Hazel and me, besides the structural problems with the building, the fact that much of the warfare had occurred at the manse made it a difficult place to live.

It remained on the market for a period of time with no expressions of interest. One person showed up. He politely walked through the house and left, but we are convinced that he had just gotten lost and was too embarrassed to admit it. The only other person who viewed the house appeared less than impressed.

During 2011, and just before the manse went up for sale, I came across a book, *Angels on the Walls*, about an Anglican church whose vicar was Wallace Brown. He had gone to a church with a congregation of a scant twenty people in a very rundown housing estate in Quinton, Birmingham. The comparisons between this church and Scrabo intrigued me.

In the book, Brown talked about how the manse had been the focus of spiritual warfare. He had done something that I had not considered, even though Hazel had. He writes:

> The very next day, Mary and I went out and prayed on location, feeling slightly foolish, I asked God to place Guardian Angels all around the walls to make them safe, to bring Godliness to our lawns and boundaries. It felt good, the effect was immediate and astonishing. Within a few days the gang started to break up, from the 35 swearing, screaming youths of the previous week, the numbers dropped by about ten

and then by the following week a mere two or three. Mary and I continued to go out and pray day by day, "Lord, keep your guarding angels around these walls please."

This manse was the scene where gangs of thirty or forty from the estate climbed its wall and fought during the night. As a result, the family of four, including the vicar, were made to feel like prisoners in their own home. The activities that had surrounded the home had left them feeling hurt, heartbroken, anxious, and fearful. Yet they had prayed specifically, and God had delivered them from the surrounding warfare. St. Boniface Church had been akin to Scrabo in so many ways. At a congregational level, they had witnessed numerical and spiritual growth. They had showed compassion while engaging with a hurting and broken community. As a people, they were passionate about pursuing God.

By 2012, our manse had been on the market for a significant period of time without being sold. We decided to contact people involved in prayer ministry and experienced in spiritual warfare to come and pray for the house. I did not agree theologically with everything they did or even said. Nevertheless, Hazel and I believed that something that could not be accounted for solely in terms of the recession was hindering the sale of the manse. Both Hazel and I felt that the physical property had become a tangible reminder of dark moments and unhappy experiences. If there was ever such a thing as post traumatic stress related to a property, this was it!

We may have fought and won some battles there, but their lingering effect still drained us, and perhaps Satan was all too aware of that. In essence we wanted to leave this particular battlefield, but no one seemed interested in purchasing it from us. So we invited people more experienced than us to pray that we would be released from the spiritual effects of living there.

We made sure that the children were elsewhere that evening when the team arrived. They asked our permission to pray for the property, knowing that it had been the focal point of spiritual warfare. To my surprise they quietly and without drama (although I am not sure what I was expecting) prayed for the house. In short, they asked God to remove any lingering effects of these battles. I had mixed emotions when they left. I had been concerned that they would be extreme, and to my surprise they had been quite subdued. But I was nonetheless encouraged that they had shown us compassion and prayerful support. However, I was somewhat surprised to God's immediate response to at least one of those prayers.

A few days later, someone came to view the property. They put an offer on it. However, wouldn't it be nice if life just went according to our plans and expectations!

While all of this was going on, I felt that to enter a new phase of ministry at Scrabo, I had to explore a new way of moving forward. With this in mind, I rang the Vicar of St. Boniface's and said: "Reverend Yates, you will not know me from Adam, but I am a Presbyterian minister in Ireland working on the Westwinds Housing Estate in a church called Scrabo Presbyterian. I just want to ask you one question that has concerned me for some period of time. Has your church continued to grow, or has it declined? I know it is a rather bold question."

"You know, Alistair, the congregation lay vacant for a few years, but it continued to grow even during the vacancy. Such was the foundation laid that it flourished even without a vicar."

I wanted to learn more about this church. "Listen, can I come and see it?"

"By all means. If you come over, you can stay in the community if you want."

So I applied for my sabbatical entitlement, upped sticks, and went to live in Quinton for a week so that I could see how that church was operating in the middle of a housing estate.

My initial impression was sheer admiration, impressed by the number of professional people connected with the church who had chosen to live on the housing estate when they could have lived in a much nicer and safer area. I stayed with a lady whose late husband had been the joint partner of a law firm in Birmingham. She had been living in this disadvantaged community for over twenty years. She was an Oxford graduate and considered it a privilege and calling to remain there.

A young couple invited me to their house for tea. He was a head of department in one of the local academy schools, and she was a Cambridge graduate. They had decided they wanted to bring up their family on the housing estate. The next day I spoke with a newly married couple who had just purchased a house on Welsh Farm, the adjoining estate. This area was equally, if not more, socially deprived than Quinton. She was a teacher and her husband had a well-paying job. They believed that if they wanted to worship in the local church, they should also live in the local community. I thought, "What a brilliant testimony to a church engaged in the community, that people were prepared to forego a more comfortable living so they could be closer to the people they wanted to reach."

I returned to Scrabo, fired up and excited about the possibility of reigniting community engagement.

The past couple of months had been eventful for other reasons too. During that time three conveners approached me to consider applying for their vacant congregations. Hazel and I prayed through each of these situations and felt that the answer to all of them was no. Thankfully, we at last felt God wanted us to prepare for another period of ministry with the people we had fallen in love with.

CHAPTER TWENTY-ONE

Standing in the Midst of Fire

It was not long until I developed a passion for community engagement. I found that it wasn't difficult to fall in love with the people who lived in the Westwind. But, like before, God had been the source behind all such initiatives.

Just a few months after my encounter with God in the

link corridor, I was attending the Christian Resource Exhibition being held in the King's Hall, Belfast. Michael Taylor, then Housing Manager for the Housing Executive in Ards, approached me. "Alistair, we've had some real difficulties engaging the community on housing issues. Is there any way you would consider trying to help as the minister of that community?"

I gave it some thought. "Okay, maybe that is something I could be involved in."

After discussing the proposition with a few elders who lived on the housing estate, I decided to take up Michael's offer. I believed that vocalising our concerns to provide better housing for residents was an extension of the principle "love thy neighbour as thyself." The points system used by the Housing Executive to allocate housing was new to me, but I learned quickly how it operated. I also became aware of the tensions between housing vulnerable people and the existing neighbours. Bringing into the neighbourhood people who may engage in antisocial behaviour puts those communities at a greater risk. It is essential that if the church is to be salt and light, we must negotiate on behalf of the vulnerable, as well as respect and protect the rights, safety, and well-being of everyone.

The traditional Eleventh Night bonfire is always a colourful and merry pageant! The very first one I attended on the housing estate was exactly six months after I had arrived at Scrabo Presbyterian as their new minister. As the embers flickered against the night sky, shadowy figures emerged from the crowd. Donning masks, several loyalists, those loyal to the

United Kingdom, lifted their rifles towards the night sky and fired a volley of shots. These guys obviously wanted everyone to know of their presence. As the cheers of their supporters subsided, they blended into the background. The partying and drinking carried on as usual. I couldn't help but ask myself, "How can we celebrate something the community considers important if, albeit inadvertently, we alienate sections of it?"

A few days later I asked to have a meeting with community representatives to discuss this issue. It was my first time gathering with loyalist representatives to discuss unity within the estate. They agreed to meet, but where and when was a big question mark. I decided that the best place to meet was a room in the church. Originally, I thought we should convene on the Sunday night after all our parishioners had left the evening service. On reflection, I realised that I did not want to hide what I was doing but instead befriend everyone on the estate, regardless of lifestyle. We planned to meet at the close of church, as soon as I had finished greeting each attendee.

As I was standing at the door shaking hands with the people, I spotted the representatives' car parked in the lay-by close to church. As the few stragglers said their good-byes to me at the door, the men emerged from their car and headed towards the church. One of them said to me as he walked through the car park, "I hope you can guarantee our safety in here." It was his way of breaking the ice.

I retorted, "The last person you want to upset is my boss." He accepted this in the spirit it was intended. However, these guys were the gatekeepers of the community, and little, if anything, happened without their approval. Scrabo Presbyterian sat in the midst of a loyalist housing estate, where house evictions, punishment beatings, shootings, and even murder had been the sad tale of post-conflict Ireland. Yet I genuinely desired to help and find a way forward.

I was a little surprised by their opening remarks, considering our lighthearted exchange just minutes previous. One of the group, obviously its spokesperson, tilted towards me and said, "No one tells us what to do on this estate."

I assured them that I had no intentions of moralising or sitting in judgement. I just wanted to understand what made them tick; why they felt the need to engage in shows of strength. I guaranteed that I had no plan of telling them what to do. I asked, "Do you think I could be a loyalist, too?" I am not sure they were entirely expecting this turn in the conversation.

I promised them that if we could create more of a community atmosphere at these public events, like Eleventh Night, I would bring my family down the following year. A few weeks later they sent word that next years' bonfire would have no shows of strength. I kept my word, and almost every year after, my family or I joined them at their Eleventh Night bonfire.

Maybe you're questioning my presence at such festivals, seeing it as an endorsement of sectarian practices. I do not share this perspective; rather, I see it as an opportunity to be salt and light in a dark world. We are all sinners saved by God's grace regardless of where we stand or even sit. Sinners may be standing at a bonfire or beside you in the Rugby club.

God doesn't make the same distinctions about sinners that we are tempted to make. Jesus referred to some religious leaders as whitewashed sepulchres. Inherently self-righteous, these leaders sanitised their own sins whilst being particularly harsh regarding other people's transgressions. The same Pharisaic spirit can so easily affect us all.

I remember a radio presenter asking me, "It is well known within the community that you sit down with those involved in criminal activity. How can you justify that as a Presbyterian minister?"

Good question. I answered clearly and unequivocally. "I have always sat down with people who have been involved in activities that may have ended in a custodial sentence. I have met rich, well-respected people who have been involved in tax evasion. Am I to sit with only those deemed respectable in society, even though they, too, have committed a crime, but shun others within this community considered less respectable? If you are making a distinction between crimes that not even the courts recognise, why should I make the same distinctions between people? However, such reservations about endorsement are flawed. Genuine dialog involves sharing our differences. On many occasions, my involvement was to offer a different perspective and alternative pathway, not a justification or endorsement of their practices or illegal activities. If that voice is not heard, how can societies change?

"I have one further observation. If many of the evangelicals had stayed around the bonfires and not moved out of housing estates in the 1970s and 1980s, then perhaps the salt and light would have had transformed those communities. I understand why they did leave, and it is an observation rather than a judgement; however, it is ironic that we moved our families to safety but prayed that God would protect our missionaries who are in dangerous environments. Perhaps, and I use the word *perhaps* because I cannot know with certainty, if we had remained and helped redeem our cultures, then the vacuum would not have been filled by those with what many regard as less noble aims."

Remember, the devil is a creature of violence. How could we resist the Enemy's presence in those communities when we effectively retreated to the safety of the suburbs? Raising a white flag, we left without a fight. We not only gave him a foothold, we left the door wide open. All these years later, my postulations can be only speculative. I can't help but think it might have been different had we stayed put.

On that dark Sunday evening as I sat surrounded by loyalists, a new light dawned, and the spirit of opportunity grabbed my heart. I joined the Westwinds Development Association (WWDA) and threw my heart and soul behind it. I felt so much a part of this community. They were my people and their issues were my issues. It didn't matter if that issue was poor housing, loss of education, antisocial behaviour, domestic violence, or fuel poverty. These were not just social issues but deeply spiritual ones as well. Social inactivity was no longer an option for me. To be truly spiritual in this community meant that I had to be truly social. Christ had died for the entire person, and I wanted the whole person restored. Naïve, perhaps, but it was more than a bonfire that ignited my heart and still burns fiercely.

The WWDA had some tough discussions, moments of laughter, and a few setbacks. As Margaret, Jimmy, Billy, Sammy, Paul, and others discussed the problems and opportunities that lay before us, we had to put our differences behind us. Many within the community worked tirelessly to provide better housing, reduce violence, and raise healthcare awareness. We fought hard to provide facilities for children and teenagers, as well as to make sure that issues of mental health were properly understood and addressed, and that crisis aid was delivered to those most in need. I really did want our little community to be a better place to live. Whatever gains we made then could not have been achieved without the support of the voluntary and statutory agencies. My part within the big picture was very small, but it was a big privilege with lasting effects.

CHAPTER TWENTY-TWO

Standing in the Midst of Conflict

Eventually, the church began to win the confidence of the community. We showed that putting "bums on pews" was not our objective. Of course, never in doubt was that we wanted the people to gain salvation. We presented an evangelical message, method, and lifestyle that demonstrated our centrality to that core purpose. Over time, some members of the community realised that we Christians weren't there to moralise or always preach a sermon. If we wanted our sermons to be influential, it was because the condition of their lives mattered.

Love that grew from this desire to bring salvation to people's souls meant that we wanted to put food in their cupboards as well. Yet what was the point of a full stomach if you had been summoned to a punishment beating, a violence carried out against those involved in antisocial behaviour? We wanted to mediate if we could, to find ways of reducing antisocial behaviour and all its associated repercussions.

Such mediation in the midst of conflict often took days and weeks to resolve. The community invited us in, and we were not going to reject their welcome.

Working late one evening, I was about to close the shutters of the community house. From the other side of the car park a lone figure walked towards me. I recognised him as a respected community leader. It was about 7 p.m. and it had been a long day. I had the feeling it was about to get a whole lot longer.

"Alistair, where are you going?" he asked.

"I am going home."

"No, you are not. You are going back in."

"Why is that?"

"Two people have been ordered to meet here, as they have been knocking lumps out of each other over the weekend. As a result, the families are going to go to war tonight unless we do something to avert it. We got to make sure that we sort things out."

As the two guys in conflict walked into the community house, we closed and locked the doors. We seated them at opposite ends of the table. The rest of us sat somewhere in between. One of the mediators clearly outlined rules for talking and would make sure that any infringement would be met with the expected disapproval. As you can guess, the discussion got heated several times, but we were successful at diffusing the situation. It turned out that the two men's fighting had been a smoke screen for deeper divisions emanating from an incident years previous. It also came to light that alcohol had fuelled the conflict. In an attempt for a cooling off period and to avoid further confrontation, we placed a drinking ban on them both. They were not to be found in the same bars, and "doormen" enforced their compliance.

Deal done and we all could go home happy. I might even get my Chinese takeaway after all. Yet I remained curious. I turned to the man who had spoken to me earlier in the car park. "Why did you involve the church in this?"

"Because we believe that the church is fair and honest."

His response thrilled me! These community gatekeepers had embraced us right into their hearts and allowed us access into their disputes. They realised we were not out for self-glory but desired people to have a better life, free from hatred, conflict, and revenge. If they had taken a huge risk to trust us, then we must avoid giving them any reason for such a trust to be broken.

I would soon be thrust into a situation that would put this trust to the test.

CHAPTER TWENTY-THREE

Standing Up in a Protest

Oftentimes, engagement with the community required us to make very difficult decisions. The most difficult one for me arose just before I left Scrabo. It required a constructive conclusion, and it was the final time God would use me within the community.

It was the time of the flags dispute. To those not

familiar with our political context, the dispute arose when the national flag of our country was removed from city hall in Belfast. The Union Jack could now be flown only on designated days. The loyalist community felt that this was a further erosion of their links to the United Kingdom. Emotions were running deep in the Province, and opinions were deeply divided. A demonstration had been organised in the Market Square in Newtownards as part of a nationwide protest.

I received a text from a community leader: "I would like you to address the crowd in the Market Square this evening and pray for them."

I froze. The question in my mind was how to deal with this. I texted back: "I don't think I could do that."

His one-line response penetrated my heart: "I thought leaders were supposed to lead."

The message was a knife driven into my heart. "Lord, how can I lead in this situation since I am not in control of it? If things go miserably wrong and it erupts in violence, I will not only be under the scrutiny of my local church, but it may bring my whole denomination into disrepute."

I had a lot of hard thinking to do—and fast. I discussed it with the community leader. He was sympathetic that the Market Square was outside my jurisdiction; it would involve churches in the town and I would be overstepping my mark. However, if I addressed and prayed for the protestors on the estate, then perhaps this would work.

The concept of what he wanted "to work" was one of the biggest challenges to my ministry. Why was he afraid?

Why did he want me to pray? His reasoning was clear. He may or may not have believed in God. If he did, he certainly did not feel at home in church. However, he knew that I not only believed in God but also in prayer. He also was aware that this protest could end in violence. People who were attending the protest were eager to jump at the first opportunity to engage with the police. The leader genuinely did not want it to end in violence, or the protest to dissolve into chaos. If I prayed, maybe there would be no violence and it would pass off peaceably. No pressure there!

So I rang my Clerk of Session, Wallace Moore. "Wallace, I have been approached to pray and to address the crowd. What do we do?"

He was very supportive and listened closely. "I will join with you as the Clerk of Session."

We discussed it more and agreed to go to the shops, stand with the crowd, chat with them, and finally address them and pray.

At the demonstration, the flags fluttered in the wind, as did my heart. The community leader spoke to the crowd, "Alistair is here. He wants to talk to you, then he is going to pray with you."

I began by saying, "I understand the frustration you feel. You believe that your identity is being eroded, and you feel passionately about that. You have a right to voice those concerns, but I really don't think you should express those opinions aggressively or act violently towards any other individual tonight, even if you feel provoked. Now I know how difficult it is to walk away when provoked. If you are asking if

I think you have the strength to do that, my answer must be an honest no, I don't think you have the strength to walk away. But I do know Someone who could help. He could, if you are willing, enable you to walk away from any provocation or acts of violence. We are going to pray to him and ask that he will give each one of us the strength to do just that." So we prayed. It was the only time I ever received a round of applause for a prayer.

I then said, "Once you go out onto the Comber Road and begin to walk towards the town, we can't join you, as you will be involved in an illegal parade. However, what Wallace and I can do is make ourselves available, along with other community leaders, once you are in the Market Square and try to make sure that the peace is upheld."

Once we were positioned in the Market Square, the Area Commander of the Policing Service for Northern Ireland approached us. He and the Community Sergeant spoke with us. "There are a few boys beginning to block the road. If you can chat with them and encourage them to move up into the Square, that will keep one lane of traffic open. If this can be done, I will avoid reading out the Public Order Act. We don't want to fuel this situation; any way that this could be diffused would be considered very helpful."

So Wallace and I, along with the marshals, engaged in conversation with these young lads who were, thankfully, very compliant. They moved up into the Market Square, keeping the traffic free flowing.

It was the longest hour of my life, because I don't usually pray for hours, but that day I was praying constantly throughout the event, "Lord, keep this peaceful." I so much wanted these guys to realise that God answers our prayers. I believe God listened that night; therefore, the prospect of violence had been averted.

At the end of the evening the Community Sergeant approached us and said, "Alistair, who could we write to?"

"What do you mean 'write to'?"

"Your bosses at headquarters."

"Why would you feel the need to do that?"

"We believe, along with everybody else, that the church's presence here tonight meant that nobody got hurt. It's just a pity that more churches were not doing this kind of thing."

Wallace and I felt that was a tremendous affirmation of our salt and light mentality.

A few years later, a journalist asked me a question that troubled me. She was interviewing me about the Haass talks. During the interview, she became aware of my involvement in the flags dispute. Whilst she accepted that my involvement had been well intentioned, she asked, "Had the parade been given approval by the legal authorities?" Of course, they hadn't. The parade was, in fact, an illegal parade. By inference she was questioning my involvement in the protest. I soon realised that in any kind of situation in which we intersect with actual or perceived unlawful activities, or are involved at some level with unsavoury people or environments, we may face an entirely different set of questions. These questions are not only important but need to be answered

It reminded me of a dilemma I had faced at the

beginning of my community ministry. The dilemma involved just how much community information I should be in possession off. To protect personal safety, integrity, and effectiveness, it is important to have a protocol of engagement when working with those alleged to have been involved in criminal activity. As relationships develop and trust is built, without those protocols I could be forced into sharing information that could compromise my integrity. As a result, I might be considered an informant, and then personal safety and that of my family is put at risk. As a pastor, my effectiveness would be greatly diminished because the element of trust has been compromised. Alternatively, if the policing authorities know that I have strict parameters as to what knowledge I have access to, they will not be suspicious as to what I might or might not know. This unique position would allow me to work effectively with both "sides" to be trusted by both and to minister to both.

The problem was that I had no way of determining what ethical principles should govern my engagement, which carried risks. So much so that I had a series of locks fitted at the manse: one to the backdoor, and one further lock fitted on an internal door, making access to the staircase and the bedrooms more difficult.

The journalist's question (Is the price of disengaging higher than the risk of involvement?) deserved an honest thoughtful response. At an intuitive level, the answer seemed obvious. If the demonstration had collapsed into violence, the wisdom of my decision may indeed have been under scrutiny. I had believed that the community leader's request came from a genuine desire to allow people to express their opinion but in a nonviolent way. If I had refused and police officers and members of the community had been hurt or hospitalised, our belief in the power of God would have been questioned. If I had refused, the community and even the police would have taken that to mean one of two things: that Wallace and I put our reputation above the safety of others, or that we ourselves did not believe that God was interested in the request or capable of answering it. As it was, God did listen, he answered our request, and the protest went peaceably and without incident.

At Scrabo, we had taken risks with our reputation, but we also learned to be generous with our possessions. When words fail to impress, love in action, rather than pious platitudes, may convince the sceptic. We believed it important to protect people on the streets while knowing that no one is fit to fight on an empty stomach. Before Christians Against Poverty (CAP) became popular in Newtownards, we expressed this generosity through the Mustard Seed project.

Each month we gathered in long-life food provisions and put together what we called Crisis Aid, which supplied a family in need with three days' worth of food. For several years we supported thirty-plus families with food and provisions each month. This rotated depending upon those families referred to us or those we identified as in need. Over the years we must have helped hundreds of families. In monetary terms, this equated to between £800 and £1000 a month—no small feat for a congregation of 140.

Whilst Phylis headed up the Mustard Seed Project,

Carol took responsibility for supporting Woman's Aid. Each woman gathered a willing band of volunteers who lovingly packaged the necessary items. Many victims of domestic violence must leave their homes in a hurry, typically with very little with which to provide for themselves and their children. Our provisions included toiletries, baby blankets, clothing, and toys. Every package contained a simple message: "Receive this with the love of God. Sent by Scrabo Presbyterian."

In both the Mustard Seed Project and Women's Aid, love and compassion were the only motivations. We did not compel the people we ministered to come to church; there were no strings attached. The Mustard Seed Project enabled genuine and authentic relationships to be formed within the community, and those receiving support from Women's Aid knew that someone cared for them. On a number of occasions, we received drawings from the children as a thank-you for our support. I ask you, what more reward did we need?

CHAPTER TWENTY-FOUR

Standing with Others in Their Brokenness

The pain of daily life is all too apparent, and as much as we would like to shield ourselves from sorrow and troubles, we are powerless to do so. Tragedy and heartache are no respecters of persons. A day that begins in laughter can end in tears. And some people seem to have a harder life than most.

I had never met the woman, but that didn't matter. The community knew her well and all were concerned for her.

Her son had been to a party, and as a result of an incident that took place there, he had slipped into a coma. As I do in all such situations, I brace myself, ask for strength, and make my way on to the hospital ward. As I approached her, my quick assessment indicated that she was fairly young woman. Her pain was evident by her lost and bewildered demeanour. She seemed to fold into herself as she sat at the bedside of her son. Earlier that day, he had been resuscitated, and his body was making involuntary thrashing movements, apparently indicative of extensive brain damage. The prospects of recovery were poor. If he showed no improvement over the next few days, the doctors would assess the viability of keeping him on life support. It was painful to watch, and I could find no words of comfort to offer the despondent mother in this unthinkable situation. We sat silently together.

Then suddenly the circumstances changed. While the young man continued to thrash, the doctors noted signs of brain activity. Hope was birthed. If he made steady progress, then the doctors were cautiously optimistic that he would make at least a partial recovery.

Two weeks later and back from holiday, I went to visit the young man. I was astonished to find him sitting up in bed, eating yogurt, and talking. Thank God. God is good. As a consequence of the brain damage, he was left partially sighted, but he was alive and would live a relatively normal life —and that's what mattered. Without coercion, his mum started to attend church.

Not many years after her son's crisis, the woman's seven-year-old daughter contracted TB meningitis.

I went to the hospital. She was a lovely little girl. Her mum was obviously distressed. The medical professionals were doing all they could to reverse the situation, but it became apparent that they could do nothing more. The family was told to prepare for the worst.

After visiting with the mother and attempting to offer support, I left the hospital and went home. The following day I was driving slowly behind a hearse. Being laid to rest was a thirty-nine-year-old lady, a young mother leaving behind two children, neither of whom had yet reached their teens. It was a tragic scene. My heart was with the family, particularly the children, but my mind was elsewhere. It was drifting back to the sick children's unit at the Royal Victoria Hospital, Belfast. I pictured the young girl stricken with meningitis lying motionless in the bed. I could only think of the unspeakable pain her family was experiencing.

My mobile rang, jolting me out of my thoughts. The young girl's mum spoke, her voice sounding almost mechanical, as if to detach herself from the reality of her message. "The hospital is talking about turning the machine off now."

I felt torn. I wanted to be with the family as they walked this path of anguish, but I also had the funeral to attend. With as much sensitivity I could muster, I said, "I am travelling to Roselawn Funeral Home, but as soon as I can, I will be with you. Ask them not to turn the machine off until I arrive."

After the parents said their painful good-byes, we walked the corridor together. In trying to provide some solace, trying to justify God's involvement, I said something I regret even to this day. "She is in a better place now."

The mother turned to me, her eyes red and brimming with tears. "What good is that to me?"

She was right. I immediately apologised. "I was just struggling for something to say. I just have no words for this."

In my mind, I often revisit that hospital room. What I said that day was true, but it was the wrong time to say it. I no longer feel the need to explain God's actions, particularly when I haven't been asked to. I was not invited into that situation to offer a thesis on the sovereignty of God; rather, I was to demonstrate God's love and grace. It was possibly my actions rather than my words that day that revealed his presence. I learned that in heartbroken moments, silence means more than a thousand well-crafted words.

That moment also taught me something about the love of God. Not in the attempt to reconcile the death of a seven-year-old with a God who claims to be compassionate, but rather a compassionate God who sustains people regardless if they believe in him or not. This lady claimed no Christian profession. She had made no confession to faith, no promise to live the life that we presume honours God. Yet he chose to be gracious towards her. He is sovereign, after all. He bestows what is called "common grace" on the just and the unjust, the believer and the sceptic. My words that day could not have kept her from the edge of despair, but his grace would. One day I pray that his grace will take her all the way to the cross and beyond.

Many of us have experienced that silence in our lives.

Faced with the injustice and tragedy of death, we have nothing to say. As a pastor I have learned that silence, at times, can be my only response.

When she was thirteen years old, Janice lost her mother. Her brother died a short two years later. I first met her after the news of her husband's death. He was only forty years old, and killed in a tragic car accident. As we paid tribute to him at the funeral, I was conscious of her agonising loss. She was not a church attender, but had welcomed me into her home on several occasions. Surrounded by her three children, together they grieved their loss. Janice's childhood bereavement aggravated her present grief.

A few years later, Janice's son went missing. The young lad was only seventeen and had been out with friends. He had decided to go for a walk on his own, but had not returned home. His mother became anxious when she realised he was missing. The community was alerted. I called to offer comfort, reassured Janice he probably spent the night with friends oblivious to her worry. Although Janice informed the police, they told her he had not been missing long enough for the national public to be alerted.

Residents of the housing community searched night and day, until he was officially recognised as a missing person. Janice asked me to speak on national television on behalf of the family. We sat together in the interview room while the press officer briefed me on how to address the television crew. Nervous at the prospect of staring down a camera lens, my heart fluttered. As I took a deep breath to slow my heart rate, the door opened. A man in uniform signalled to the female police officer to exit the room. They returned a few minutes later. When I saw their facial expressions, my heart sank.

"A spotter helicopter has noticed a body in the water. We can't identity if it is a teenager or adult, but we have sent our ground team in to take a look," the female officer softly explained. "I will leave you with your pastor until we can investigate a little further."

The door gently closed behind me. It was the longest silence I have ever experienced. I had no words to comfort her, nothing to say. Silently we embraced each other. Glancing at each other, the windows of our soul revealed unspoken heartache. I have learned over the years that sometimes it is better just to feel empty rather than the hollow ring of mistimed words. In our grief we now simply walked together realising the toughness of the terrain.

Pastors are called upon frequently to help people walk through their various trials and tragedies. It is heartbreaking and exhausting. In these times of sorrow and grief, the preciousness of life comes into sharp focus, while the small, insignificant incidents of life fade in importance. It is this perspective of what is truly important in life that can heighten pastors' frustration when their time and energy are consumed by pointless discussions and endless debates. Being embroiled in trying to eliminate gossip and keeping both sides of the church happy. Trying to unify the church, and tiptoeing on egg shells around worship. To be sure, these discussions do have their place. But when the church distorts its priorities and engages in stupid, meaningless, and pointless distractions, we lose sight of the brokenness of our world and, most of all, the hope that it so desperately needs.

If Satan can distract us from fighting him, then at least one of his schemes has been effective. By removing his opposition, he can operate unchecked, continuing to wreak havoc on the world. A world that desperately needs the church but has at times been ashamedly deprived of its message of hope, love, and justice—the greatest story that has ever been told. Let's not deprive the world of what it needs to hear and see.

Standing in the midst of suffering reminded me that I don't have adequate words of comfort, but I have an adequate God. I have a God who will share their pain, who will walk with them, talk with them, and forever wants to be with them. It is never my sacrifice to walk with those in sorrow and grief; it is my privilege. Who has God asked you to walk with today? Show them the same compassion, grace, and patience God has shown you.

CHAPTER TWENTY-FIVE

Still Standing at the Final Bell

Debbie started to attend church. Originally, Debbie wanted to have her child baptised; however, after listening to God's Word she realised that she wasn't a Christian, therefore making her child's baptism inappropriate. Eventually she came to God but she still didn't think it right to have her child baptised. She didn't want me to think that she'd made her commitment to Christ just to have the sacrament performed.

After the church service one Sunday, she approached

me and said, "I would love you to have a talk with my husband, Steve. He hasn't been to church for years or, at least, not in any meaningful way."

I agreed to meet him. Their house was beautifully kept, with the largest television screen I have ever seen. Impressive as that was, it was the pictures on the walls that caught my attention. Steve was a professional boxer.

I have always loved boxing, and as I stared at those pictures, my mind drifted back to childhood. Boxing takes me to a happy place. I associate the noble art with my parents and the excitement of being woken up in the middle of the night and brought downstairs to watch a fight on TV. My mum was a stickler for strict bedtimes, but there were rare exceptions, and boxing was one of them. On those nights, the rules were set aside. We switched on the TV and cuddled together as a family. As the pictures beamed from across the Atlantic flickered on the screen, we were drawn into the stadium that pulsated with noise, glitz, glamour, and the anticipation as Muhammed Ali entered the ring. My mum wanted him knocked out. If ever she could have gotten near him with her handbag, she surely would've fulfilled her dream! I loved those nights. A blizzard could've been howling outside in the depth of winter, but those times with my family before the TV always left me with a warm feeling.

During my late teenage years I thoroughly enjoyed going to the Antrim Boxing Club. I was okay at sparring; and I had been in with some fairly competent fighters, some who had competed at the national level. However, boxing was frowned upon by the church, so when I got saved, it was no longer acceptable for me to box. For that reason, I didn't pursue it competitively, but I continued to love the sport.

It wasn't long until Steve and I were deep in conversation about boxing, so much that I almost forgot why I was visiting him. But church must have come into our conversation at some point because I mentioned that a Community Celebration Day was coming up and that the church was going to be involved.

Every year, the Westwinds Development Association hosted a little Celebration Day, which included various demonstrations by the Police Dog Team or the Northern Ireland Fire & Rescue Service. Burgers, hotdogs, and much more were always part of the festivities, as well as bouncy castles and a variety of other activities. It was a day to foster community spirit and raise money for a worthy charity. This particular year, we were raising money for Childhood Meningitis (TB Meningitis) in memory of the little girl who had died so tragically.

As I chatted with Steve, I said, "The church is running all of these Celebration Days, but we have really no novel way to raise money for the charity."

He eyed me. "I heard you used to box a few years ago. Why don't you box me on the estate for charity? We will do three three-minute rounds of exhibition boxing and put on a bit of entertainment for the crowd."

His idea took me by total surprise. But I was intrigued. I pondered the challenge. After some deliberation, I agreed. He assured me that although he was a professional boxer, he would go light on me. However, that bit of comfort diminished when I considered that the crowd expected to be entertained, which meant throwing and receiving punches. Though I had no illusions of defeating such a worthy foe, how could I possibly survive even a put-on beating? Steve encouraged me to come to Eastside Gym to prepare for our showdown.

I had not anticipated the community's growing interest in the upcoming fight. It seemed to gain momentum by the day.

Steve said to me one day, "It's all sorted. We are bringing a competition ring down from Belfast and will erect it in the church car park."

Now any good Presbyterian knows that shifting church furniture can cause a row, but how many committee meetings will be required to explain a boxing ring in its car park?

Steve continued. "A ring girl has been organised, and someone is going to referee it. Some lads from the gym will perform warm-up bouts, and we will be the main attraction at half past four in the afternoon."

I thought, "This is all a bit public." I felt the pressure mount.

Obviously, we thought the community would enjoy this event, but we were surprised when even the local papers showed interest. A reporter contacted me. "We have heard that that you are fighting for charity against Steve Quinn. Would you mind if we ran an article on it?"

And so they did. It was entitled "Rev. in the Ring." The opening paragraph read: "Rev. Bates is used to hearing church bells, but come this Saturday he will be coming out to bells of a different sort."

Because of this story, people outside the community heard about it and were interested in the coming bout.

After training and more assurances from Steve that he would go easy on me, I felt ready for the fight. Then when I stepped out into the car park and spotted the ambulance from St. John's, I hesitated. Hundreds of people had gathered, including some from the congregation. Elderly members took up the front row seats.

Long story, short: the bell for the first round sounded, and three rounds later I was still standing.

Stevie and I had traded punches. But it started a friendship that lasts to this day. It eventually led to baptising him, and his mum and dad came along to church not long after that. I was with Steve at the formation of Ards Boxing Club and later becoming one of its licensed boxing coaches. I enjoyed sparring, although I did end up with a fractured eye socket.

Scrabo was a wonderful parish for me because it extended into every part of living, including the boxing ring, which allowed me an opportunity to be salt and light in the community in a way that made a difference. Residents could talk to me about anything, knowing that I was a human being and not just a minister—though it certainly didn't stop them from hitting me during sparring sessions. Evidently, there is no respect for the clergy once you step under that bottom rope!

Paul declared that he had "fought the good fight,"

finished the race, and kept the faith. He was convinced that starting well was important, but finishing well was better. In life I have been up against the ropes, and some days I have looked up from the canvas. So far I have managed to beat the count. The battle has been worth every strained muscle, dark moment, and period of self-doubt. Paul once said, "Who are you to judge someone else's servant? To their own master, servants stands or fall. for the Lord is able to make them stand" (Romans 14:4). It is only because of God's grace that I find myself still standing today.

What pressures do you face? Maybe you feel pummelled by the relentless blows of life. Your vision is blurred, you are fighting back on instinct. You are far too proud to withdraw from the battle; however, if someone in your corner were to throw in the towel, you wouldn't complain, believing you'd given it your all. The Enemy has exposed your weakness and he has been ruthless in his treatment of you.

Take a deep breath, look to your corner, and stand to your feet. Others have got off the canvas before and emerged victorious, and you will do the same. Previous battles have taught you many things, but remember this: you survived them. You have everything you need to get through this, for "his divine power has given us everything we need for a godly life" (2 Peter 1:3).

You may feel exceptionally weak to do battle against the flesh, the world, and the devil. But recall that David killed Goliath, the fiercest warrior, with only a sling. Gideon gained victory over a well-armed army with only three hundred men supplied with clay pots. You might doubt your ability, but so did Moses, yet he succeeded against Pharaoh and his army. David, Gideon, Moses, and more "ill-equipped" saints made their way into the "hall of faith" of Hebrews 11. Look forward to the day when Christ raises your arms aloft in victory. When you will be listed among the great overcomers. On that day you will forget your troubles, scars, and battle wounds. What you had to endure will mean nothing in comparison with seeing Jesus's nail-pierced hands. The Redeemer will wipe away all tears from your eyes, and for the first time, with absolute clarity, you will see how he carried you from the canvas to the crown.

CHAPTER TWENTY-SIX

Still Trading Punches

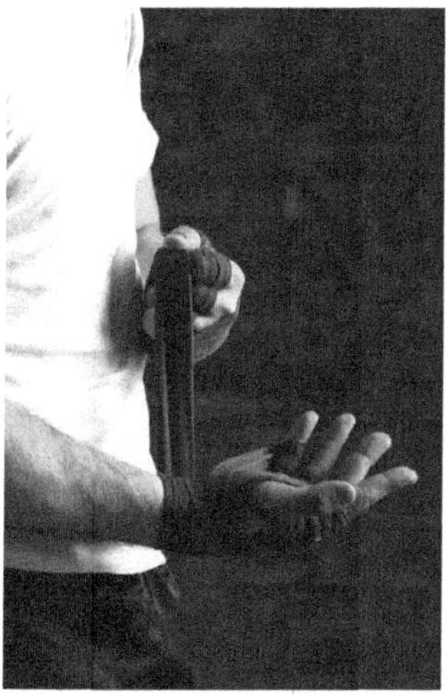

What is the point in my story unless I can trace God's hand across the pages of my life? As I look back I can still feel what it was like to be without God. My brokenness was not due to drugs or alcohol. I had not spent time in prison or run the streets with a criminal gang. People didn't avoid me. From appearances I looked okay. But I wasn't. The flesh, compelled and motivated by sin, had done as much to break me as it had done to those looking at the world through a whiskey glass. Deep inside a war raged, and it was winning. I had lost my aspiration for life and for a future. I was drowning, and, sadly, few could see it. My parents did and perhaps some of my closest friends, but the one I needed to see it most was God. I thank God that he did.

When God looks at you he sees more than skin and bone. He sees more than a broken body, and he laments over a broken life. The gospel is about God stepping in. It's about the cross and Jesus dying for your sin and mine. It is about Jesus taking the penalty for sin so that you don't have to. It truly is about God saving you. The day that he saved me, my recovery began. I thank God he was the only one who could transform my life, and I believe with all my heart that he can transform yours. If he can use me to do a work for him, he can certainly use you.

Before I step into the pulpit to preach, I kneel to pray. This is no empty ritual. It reminds me that I am here because he took a broken life and is repairing it. It reminds me, that the message I am about to deliver can change lives. It reminds me that God creates ex nihilo (out of nothing); therefore, he can repair the most bankrupt of lives. You might feel as if you have nothing to give, that you are not as talented or gifted as others around you. But it's not your giftedness, certificates, money, or status he requires. It is simply just you. And it's all of you that he wants, including the broken bits you haven't been able to fix.

Even after God has rescued us, weakness remains because it keeps us dependent on God. As I look back over my life and remember some of its pain, I have a choice to make, as do each of us. We can choose to be bitter and resentful, or we can choose to see the fingerprints of God's redemptive plan. One day God will hold accountable those who hurt you, but it may not be today. Why put your life on hold until that day happens? No matter how difficult this may be, we have got to see God's fingerprints imprinted on the pages of our lives. Though we may need some forensic dust to help us see them, they are there.

I have asked God to baptise my memories, and he is helping me wash them clean. It is not easy, and some days it's more difficult than others because I am a work in progress, as are you. Be patient, he hasn't finished with you yet. The fight against the flesh, the world, and the devil is rarely won in the first round. This is a fight to the final bell. Be patient. Some rounds you may lose, but that is very different from loosing the fight. Stay in there. God is in your corner.

Perhaps you have been trying to beat the flesh, world, and devil in your own strength. If you have, then stop now. You won't win. Remember, the flesh is a life disorientated from God. Trying to live the Christian life independent of God is impossible. Satan's desire is to create distance between God and his people. When we see that happening, we need to take James 's advice, "Come near to God and he will come near to you. Wash your hands, you sinners, and purify your hearts, you double-minded. Grieve, mourn and wail. Change your laughter to mourning and your joy to gloom. Humble yourselves before the Lord, and he will lift you up" (James 4:8). Once we admit that we want our lives reorientated to God, he will lift us up.

God longs for the Holy Spirit to be at work in our lives. The work of the Spirit is the only remedy to a life under pressure from the flesh, the world, the devil and demonic forces. James writes, "Or do you think Scripture says without reason that he jealously longs for the spirit he has caused to dwell in us? But he gives us more grace. That is why Scripture says:

> God opposes the proud
> but shows favor to the humble. (James 4:5-6)

To fight this war, to have victory in his work, to make it to the final bell, we need to be filled with the Holy Spirit. The opposite of the manifestation of the flesh is the demonstration of the fruit of the Spirit. Paul declares, "But the fruit of the Spirit is love, joy, peace, forbearance, kindness, goodness, faithfulness, gentleness and self-control. Against such things there is no law" (Galatians 5:22–23). What a wonderful blessing we would be to the world around us if we came under the control of the Spirit. One of the greatest chapters that encourages us to live by the power of the Spirit, in our war against the flesh is Romans 8. Why not take a few moments and prayerfully reflect on that passage?

When I began my ministry in Scrabo, I was convinced that God worked within the parameters of my own theological assumptions. Reacting against my earlier charismatic/

Pentecostal experiences, I had limited God. However, engagement with the world and demonic forces reminded me that the war in which we are engaged is a spiritual war, so at times God will use extraordinary, not extra-biblical, means of gaining our attention or reminding us of his power. Are you limiting God today, or do you need to be reminded that he is sovereign? Signs and wonders follow the preaching of the Word and are particularly evident when that declaration is made while depending on the power of the Holy Spirit. I am dismayed by those who are obsessed with the miraculous, as if there is not enough evidence of God in his church or the world around them. Nevertheless, living the Christian life is a supernatural experience, and why should we not expect God to move in supernatural ways?

Living in the Spirit requires us to take risks, to break free from our holy huddle, and venture out into a world of chaos. We must take seriously the Great Commission. Luke reminds us in Acts 13:47, "For this is what the Lord has commanded us:

> "I have made you a light for the Gentiles,
> that you may bring salvation to the ends of the earth."

It is clear what our passion and priorities should be. The world is broken and needs us. If we are not salt and light, then moral restraint and influence upon the world is weakened, and the lies of the Enemy drown out the message of the gospel. If this book is to achieve anything, it is to inspire us to believe that God changes us, and in the process we are inspired to believe the world can be changed too. Such changes do not come from putting together mission strategies or well-intentioned programs. They call us to leave the safety of conference desks, church pews, and comfortable armchairs and make our way into a heartbroken world that needs us to bring the message of Christ. There we will cry and bathe the wounds of the bleeding. We will venture into the dark corners and murky side streets until the light of the gospel shines, and we are finally liberated from the war against the flesh, the brokenness of this world, and destructive powers of the Evil One. That day is coming soon Paul declares, very soon. Make these final rounds of trading punches your championship rounds where you see "the God of peace crush Satan under your feet" (Romans 16:20).

AFTERWORD

Though no longer Scrabo's minister, a piece of my heart remains with the people. I want Scrabo to continue to flourish. I know in my heart of hearts that the current minister, Aaron Ditty, has gifts I do not possess, and he can take Scrabo Presbyterian to places that are far beyond where I could.

When I arrived at Scrabo, David and Anne, John and Sally, and John Doc were key figures in the life of the congregation. David stood with me through one of my greatest trials, and I am not sure even he fully appreciated how much that meant to me.

One of the saddest tasks of ministry is having to bury those whom you love. I buried both David and John, and their deaths not only hit their families hard but also the Scrabo family. Their legacy ripples through the congregation today. These men bore cancer with a courage that only faith can bring, but today with joy and without pain, they worship in heaven the God they so tirelessly served on earth.

As an entire congregation, we nervously set out on a

journey that became an adventure. Three previous ministers and an entire congregation had given years of service not only to the church but, more important, to their loving Master.

Moving out into community, with Margaret Cameron, Paul Simpson, and others, saved me from the introspection of church ministry. And, as a result, breathed new life into my heart and soul. Now as the Spirit continues to empower Aaron's ministry, I await with expectation to one day read of his adventures too.

Chapters are yet to be written. For me it is no longer at Scrabo; however, my story must not end there. I am in Wellington now, a very different place and an altogether different challenge, but the same God leads me. I never want the adventure to end.

Thank God, he answered my mum's prayer. I never wanted to become a Christian, let alone go into the ministry. But if I hadn't, I would never have had the privilege of seeing God do the things he did—and is still doing.

I may still be standing today by God's grace, but I am also still striving and pressing forward to the goal. One day we will stand together, raise our hands aloft, and sing, "Worthy! Worthy is the Lamb who takes away the sin of the world." We may feel battered, but it's time to fight back. With God's help, we can trade punches with the flesh, the world, and the devil —and, thankfully, win.

Notes

Chapter Two

1. Steven L. Porter, "The Gradual Nature of Sanctification: σάρξ, as Habituated, Relational Resistance, to the Spirit," *Themelios*, Vol. 39, No. 3, November 2014, 474–75.

2. Gregory A. Boyd, *Present Perfect* (Grand Rapids MI: Zondervan, 2010), 50.

About the Author

Alistair faced a difficult childhood, as he struggled to learn at school. Only when he discovered God's love in his late teenage years did he find and develop a passion for life. The Bible was the first book he ever read meaningfully, which propelled him into lifelong education. A graduate of Queen's University Belfast, he was awarded degrees in Social Anthropology and Divinity. Currently he is undertaking his Doctorate at the University of Glasgow.

BOOKS BY THE SAME AUTHOR

Halloween, Happy Holiday or Dangerous Deception?

Halloween is not simply child's play. In this provocative exploration of fact versus fiction, Reverend Alistair Bates uncovers Halloween's historical journey from pagan origins to Christian acceptance. He examines four common responses from churches today, and calls on faith leaders to consider what is at stake when popular holidays are incorporated into

Christian belief and practice.

- Should the Church be concerned with the myths and meanings behind Halloween celebrations?
- What does the Bible say about accepting pagan practices into the Christian calendar?
- Can Halloween be redeemed or should families reject the holiday completely?

Halloween, Happy Holiday or Dangerous Deception? is an excellent resource for parents who want to raise Godly children in an ungodly world, and offers reflection questions that are useful for any Church group studying what Scripture says about the seductions of evil. This is a bold—and necessary—look at the true meanings of Halloween and how Christians can choose to counter a culture of darkness with the light of Jesus Christ.

VITAL SIGNS (BOOK 1)

Forgiveness and Paradise

Under the dark skies of Jerusalem, a drama unfolded. What appeared to be a cosmic tragedy was ironically Jesus's greatest triumph. Death's icy fingers clutched at the heart of Jesus, but they dissolved like snow in the heat of his love.

In this book series, you will discover that what appeared to be a dark, miserable, godforsaken day over Jerusalem was the most glorious of all time. During the agony of the cross, where fear, despair, and heart-pounding sadness filled the air, Jesus's dying words brought hope in the midst of despair. Jesus extended grace and hope to us all.

This story is saturated with gracc, and it reveals the possibilities of pivotal moments and life-changing encounters. Jesus extends the gift of grace to all.

It is never too late for you to experience the God of relentless grace. The cross is a story of relentless love. A picture painted large with the brushstrokes of grace. Against the backdrop of cruelty and injustice, hope rises as a defiant flare. "Today you will be with me in paradise." Oh, what grace, what love, what power to forgive, what goodness of heart! Jesus embraced a dying man and is willing to embrace each of us too. He gave reassurance to a broken man who dared to ask Jesus to remember him, and to his relief Jesus said "Yes!" Imagine the joy that Jesus's salvation brought to that criminal's heart. Forever let it bring hope and joy to yours.